JOHN WESLEY
AND
SLAVERY

JOHN WESLEY
AND
SLAVERY

WARREN THOMAS SMITH

Abingdon Press

Nashville

John Wesley and Slavery

Library of Congress Cataloging in Publication Data

SMITH, WARREN THOMAS, 1923–
John Wesley and slavery.

Bibliography: p.
Includes index.
1. Wesley, John, 1703–1791—Views on slavery. 2. Slavery and the church—Methodist Church—History—18th century. 3. Slavery and the Church of England—History—18th century. 4. Methodist Church—Doctrines—History—18th century. 5. Church of England—Doctrines—History—18th century. 6. Anglican Communion—Doctrines—History—18th century. I Title.
BX8495.W5S547   1986   261.8'34567'0924   85-15796

ISBN 0-687-20433-X
(alk. paper)

Scripture quotations unless otherwise noted are from the Revised Standard Version of the Bible, copyrighted 1946, 1952, 1971, © 1973, by the Division of Christian Education of the National Council of the Churches of Christ in the U.S.A., and used by permission.

Those noted KJV are from the King James Version.

MANUFACTURED BY THE PARTHENON PRESS AT
NASHVILLE, TENNESSEE, UNITED STATES OF AMERICA

In memory of my aunt
Jennie Deborah Jones
April 1, 1885–December 13, 1966
who, for forty-one years, 1912-1953,
served as a Methodist missionary in China.
Jane D. Jones, as she preferred to be called,
served with zeal and compassion
people of many races in many lands.
She captured the Wesley spirit,
"I look upon *all the world as my parish*,"[1]
Matthew 28:19-20

---

[1]Frank Baker, ed., *The Oxford Edition of the Works of John Wesley*, vol. 25, *Letters I, 1721-1739* (Oxford: Clarendon Press, 1980), p. 616.

John Wesley

The shades of Oxford—
The gallant More
And princely Addison—
Beckoned him to primrose paths of glory:
A peer, a premier, or a laureate.
He chose the Wyclif-way
That led to Calvary:
"A crude ecstatic!
"A Methodist!"
He took the world for his parish
And dreamed
That it could be redeemed
By faith in God,
A God,
"Who buries His workmen
But carries on His work."

Earl Bowman Marlatt, *Chapel Windows*

CONTENTS

PREFACE

*O*ne of the urgent world-wide concerns of thoughtful people is racism, linked with oppression of the poor and the powerless. It is indeed interesting that the eighteenth century might give fresh insight into this enormous, complex problem. John Wesley becomes an example of the unity of deep piety and vibrant social concern. Too often, these twin aspects of vital faith are disjoined. It is a tragic mistake. As one reads of John Wesley's long concern for African people, one is made conscious of what "world parish" really means.

My own study of Wesley goes back to grammar school; it has been, for me, a lifelong interest. My article "Sketches of Early Black Methodists" appeared in *The Journal Of The Interdenominational Theological Center*, Fall, 1981. Since beginning my teaching at the Interdenominational Theological Center, I have encouraged my students to read Wesley's *Thoughts upon Slavery,* and that has been rich and rewarding. I am now endeavoring to cite the many references by Wesley to Africans, to slavery, and to the attempts on his part to abolish the demonic trade in human flesh. One cannot fully see and hear Wesley on the subject without reading *Thoughts upon Slavery.* Thus, it is reproduced in this volume from an original in the Wesley Collection of Drew University Library.

My thanks to Professor Kenneth E. Henry of the Interdenominational Theological Center, Mr. John A.

Vickers of Bognor Regis, Sussex, England, and Professors Robert E. Smith and Arthur W. Wainwright of Emory University, who read early drafts of the manuscript and made valuable contributions. It was not until I was well along in the writing that I found Professor Frank Baker's article, "The Origins, Character, and Influence of John Wesley's Thoughts upon Slavery," in the January, 1984, issue of *Methodist History*. I am deeply in debt to Dr. Baker, Professor Emeritus of English Church History at the Divinity School, Duke University, not only for this treatise, but for his scholarly contributions throughout the years. He graciously read my manuscript and made significant suggestions. I trust this work reflects my gratitude and his help. Responsibility for content of this work, I must assume. I am appreciative of the assistance given by Mrs. Sara Mobley of Pitts Theology Library, Candler School of Theology, Emory University, in securing important Wesley material, and the staff of Special Collections of Emory's Robert W. Woodruff Library for works by Benezet. Deep appreciation is expressed to the Library of Drew University for the use of Wesley's *Thoughts upon Slavery,* reproduced in this volume.

As always, my thanks to my family: Barbara and our Warren, who deserve more credit than I can give for their sustaining spirit and loving support.

John Wesley has so much to tell us, not only respecting relations of races, cultures, and nationalities, but he also tells us about God's redemptive work in Jesus the Christ. Wesley seeks to bring it into one powerful message. It is a message we need to hear!

Warren Thomas Smith
Interdenominational Theological Center
Atlanta, Georgia
January-February 1985
The anniversary of the publication of
Thoughts upon Slavery, 211 years ago, 1774

PROLOGUE

The date was July 31, 1838. Within twenty-four hours the last technical vestiges of slavery would be officially abolished within the British Empire! Most of these were Africans, some 768,000—not counting those held by local officials: princes and sovereigns who were indeed reluctant to relinquish their chattels. It was the end of an interminable, heartrending era.[1] Parliament had passed the Emancipation Act on August 1, 1833, stipulating that all slaves were manumitted, with an appropriation of £20,000,000 to indemnify planters for the loss of their property. Slavery, as such, was thus terminated by 1834, but a transitional system of apprenticeship was to continue for another four years—a period wherein brutality, such as excessive flogging and other demeaning practices, remained. August 1, 1838, marked the discontinuance of the apprenticeship interlude.

The surprising element is that for many white English people (white Americans and other Europeans as well), there had been so little tragedy in it. After all, slavery had seemed part of the general scheme of things. Had not Aristotle insisted "from the hour of their birth, some men are marked out for subjection, others for rule"? It was part of the divine order. Boswell had maintained, "To abolish a *status*, which in all ages GOD has sanctioned, and man has continued, would not only be *robbery* to an innumerable class of our fellow-subjects; but it would be extreme cruelty to the African Savages, a portion of whom it saves from massacre, or intolerable bondage in their own country, and introduces into a much happier state of life; especially now when their passage to the West Indies and their treatment there is humanely regulated. To abolish that trade would be to '—shut the gates of mercy on mankind.' "[2]

A facade had been created in the course of three hundred years. A striking example would be the beautiful little town of Falmouth in northern Jamaica. A plantation, Orange Valley, would serve as a model of how proficiently and effortlessly the system worked:

It was built of solid limestone, and displayed an almost ecclesiastical air of conviction. On the hill above stood its Great House, balconied and wide-eaved, lapped by lawns and caressed by creepers. Nearby was the house of the overseer, an English yeoman house, pretty in an unassuming way, as though always conscious of its place at the mansion gates.[3]

This romantic, bucolic scene, so serene and idealistic, took on increased character:

And all around the central factory area, where the sugar was refined and packed, were the slave-installations—the slots or stables or repair bays in which those human mechanisms were installed, housed and serviced . . . the slave quarters were rows and rows of shanties, like rickety garden pavilions . . . . It was a highly functional arrangement: like a ship disposed about its engine-room, the estate was assembled efficiently about its motive-power, the muscle of captive humans.[4]

Here was a major problem with the whole episode of West African slavery. It had been made to appear—as in the antebellum South in the United States—as a comfortable, economically feasible, though a "peculiar institution," which was blandly accepted as a way of life. For the white slaveholder there was an aura of hauteur; for the slave, the wretchedness of subjugation and dehumanization.

Beneath the veneer, and the plantation myth, lay the reality "that British slave-masters could be as cruel as any Arab traders or Bokhara khan."

ears cut off in punishment, eyes gouged, teeth drawn, hands amputated. Slaves were hung by their arms from trees, nailed by their ears to posts, clamped in steel collars or iron boots . . . the slave had been utterly at the mercy of his employer—or worse still his employer's wife, who was often more vicious in the refinement of her spite.[5]

Little wonder that in the small Jamaican town, late at night on July 31, 1838, the Reverend William Knibb, pastor of the Baptist church, announced to the congregation which was watching the clock move toward midnight, "The hour approaches!" Then, pointing to the moving hands of the timepiece, "The time is drawing near! The monster is dying!" As the clock struck the hour, twelve times, the pastor cried, "The monster is dead!" The people were ecstatic. They chanted:

> *Now slavery we lay thy vile form in the dust,*
> *And buried for ever let it there remain!*
> *And rotted and covered with infamy's dust*
> *Be every man-whip and fetter and chain.*[6]

Bonfires had been prepared on mountain and hilltops throughout Jamaica and the entire British West Indies. As August 1, 1838, came, these fires could be seen across the Caribbean, reflecting from island to island, signaling through the warm summer night, liberation had arrived.

How did it all come to pass? Who was responsible for the eradication of this intolerable institution of slavery? Indeed, many! One name, however, must be mentioned. He contributed much more than most people have ever recognized—more than he himself ever knew. It is long past time that he received his due recognition. His name is John Wesley![7]

CHAPTER

I

SLAVERY

*I*n humankind's long, slow, tortuous rise from barbarism to civilization and on to enlightened humane society, few tragedies have inflicted so much agony as human slavery. The institution, with all its attendant malefic ramifications, is as old as the race. Appearing in a wide variety of forms, and under an assortment of technical names, slavery remains the horrid laceration on the face of human history.

Antiquity

Pharaoh in ancient Egypt held tenancy over considerable portions of the Two Lands, with thousands of peasants owing the Great House part of their labor. These early children of the Nile made slaves of prisoners taken in battle; foreigners (as in the case of the Hebrews) were often held in bondage. Vassal nations frequently sent children to Egypt as tribute—to become slaves.

At the height of Egypt's power, however, there was no domestic slave trade, as existed in Babylonia and

Assyria. In these powerful empires, entire populations were oftentimes enslaved and transported. As these nations went into decline, the exporting of slaves increased markedly; revenue was needed.

Phoenicians played no small role in spreading slavery throughout the Mediterranean world. Ancient Greece practiced involuntary servitude quite as much as the Phoenicians, as illustrated in the *Odyssey,* which describes the women of slain warriors being sold into slavery. Greek slaves were not chattel, and their treatment was reasonably lenient. Aristotle had even advocated manumission as a reward for devoted performance of duty.

In Hebrew culture, Mosaic Law insisted children born of slave parents were not free; they were victims of the conditions imposed—usually the fortunes of war— upon their parents. Exodus 21:2-11 stated the conditions whereby a slave was free after six years. (See Lev. 25:10 ff regarding the year of jubilee and the freeing of an Israelite slave.) This did not apply to strangers.

When you buy a Hebrew slave, he shall serve six years, and in the seventh he shall go out free, for nothing. If he comes in single, he shall go out single; if he comes in married, then his wife shall go out with him. If his master gives him a wife and she bears him sons or daughters, the wife and her children shall be her master's and he shall go out alone. (Exod. 21:2-4)

Ancient Rome regarded slavery as a policy of national life. A master held power of life and death over slaves. Increased wars brought enormous quantities of slaves to the City on the Tiber. On one occasion Julius Caesar seized 63,000 Gauls. Eventually Imperial Rome became stifled economically by the sheer immensity of its slave culture. Construction of magnificent public buildings, copying of books in private and public libraries, and elaborate gladiatorial spectacles, were all the work of slaves. The slave population simply became too large and too expensive.

People, both primitve and highly cultured, in large sections of Africa, in the Malay archipelago, India, Indochina, China, and Japan practiced the enslavement of human beings in one form or another. In North America, as well as in sections of Central and South America and in the islands of the Pacific, slavery was utilized. The institution was found most frequently among agricultural communities. It must be said that among primitive people, slavery was a minor issue. Tribal life tended to absorb the slave into the general population. It must also be said, "In antiquity, . . . bondage had nothing to do with physiognomy or skin color."[1]

Europe: The Middle Ages

In Medieval Europe, slavery was imposed as a consequence of war, penalties for crime, and parentage. Augustine was in many ways responsible for the attitude toward slavery. He listed four points: (1) prior to the Fall, all people were equal; (2) the Fall, and the universal sinfulness that resulted, demanded institutions of coercion; (3) masters were to be kind, and slaves obedient; and (4) the most outrageous form of slavery was sin, regardless of the individual's social or economic status.[2]

Serfdom gradually replaced slavery, and by the tenth century slavery was hardly mentioned. The worker was no longer chattel, but was required to give the lord a fixed portion of services. The serf held a few acres of the lord's land. Unlike the free peasants, serfs could not move at will; in effect, they were tied to the land. The lower classes were, by this time, usually segregated into categories: freemen who rented their farms and were required to render service to the lord, villeins who were appurtenances to the land, and serf masters.

Muslim Life

Slavery was highly specialized in Islamic nations, as in the case of thirteenth-century Egypt, where the Mamelukes, a military class originally composed of slaves, seized control of the sultanate in A.D. 1250 and ruled until 1517. The Ottoman sultan, Murad I, in the fourteenth century, maintained a formidable army of slave-warriors known as Janissaries. These had been taken as Christian children and schooled to become redoubtable soldiers. The Barbary States practiced regular raids on European ships, taking large numbers of Christian slaves. Atrocities of the Islamic slave trade became legendary.

Arabs of North Africa became middlemen in the slave trade with countries in Asia and Europe—a function they maintained for almost four hundred years. Caravans of Arabs made their way to the Gold Coast in quest of gold. From the lower Niger they obtained palm oil. By far the greatest values in the Sudanese–Central Africa territory were ivory and human beings. "The routes across the Sahara sands were strewn with the skeletons of Negroes." Vast numbers of slaves were conveyed to Persia and Arabia. Immense fortunes were amassed by these Arab traders.

West Africa

The infamous West Africa slave trade had its genesis in the fifteenth century, when Prince Henry the

Navigator of Portugal induced his daring seamen to go down the coast of Africa. The year A.D. 1441 saw a group of Negroes from Rio de Oro arrive in Lisbon. By the following year, 1442, the Portugese began making inroads into villages where they would "carry off some of the natives"[3] said Anthony Benezet.

It was Christopher Columbus' arrival, on October 12, 1492, probably at Watlings Island—which he promptly named San Salvador—in the Bahamas, and the claiming of the entire region for the Spanish crown, that ushered Spanish presence into the New World. With the blessing of the Pope, Spain soon had a hegemony in the Caribbean, Central and South America. It was an unbelievably vast territory. Gold was the object of Spanish exploration. In the Caribbean, Ciboneys, Arawaks, and Caribs were conscripted to mine the precious metal. In 1500, Hispaniola is estimated to have had a population of approximately 300,000. Within forty years, Spanish brutality, disease, and the severity of the mines and boundless fields, had virtualy exterminated that population. "This slave labor now lacking, the Spanish colonial empire in America was threatened with collapse. Blacks from West Africa were imported to replace the Indians." Thus the Spanish instituted the West Indian slave trade. "But the grandiose visions of New World wealth—once the Spanish had plundered the Aztecs and Incas—seemed always to require slave labor. The Negro slave thus became an intrinsic part of the American experience."[4] The trade grew quickly, and the number of Africans increased yearly. Blacks proved to be equal to the demanding labor. "There can be no doubt that both the Spanish and Portuguese turned to African labor as a more reliable and durable substitute for captive aborigines, who seemed in the sixteenth century to be on the path to extinction."[5]

This system proved to be highly profitable for both the Spanish and the Portuguese, as lucrative for them as it was inhuman for the Africans.[6] In 1537 alone, 10,000 Africans were shipped to Portugal. Eventually most of these people were sent to Brazil, where an enormous Portuguese empire was being created and where the largest quadrant of African slaves would be located.

England and the Slave Trade

English trading in Guinea began, says Benezet, "about the year 1551, towards the latter end of the reign of king Edward the sixth, when some London merchants sent out the first English ship, on a trading voyage to the coast of Guinea; this was soon followed by several others to the same parts." Benezet made the pertinent observation, "the English not having any plantations in the West Indies, and consequently no occasion for Negroes, such ships traded only for gold, Elephants teeth and Guinea pepper."[7]

This would soon change. In 1562, Sir John Hawkins took three hundred slaves from Sierra Leone. "Negroes are very good merchandise in Hispaniola and many Negroes might easily be had on the coast of Ghana." Worthy of note is the reaction of the English monarch, "when captain Hawkins returned from his first voyage to Africa, Queen Elizabeth sent for him, when she expressed her concern, lest any of the African Negroes should be carried off without their free consent; which she declared would be detestable, and would call down the vengeance of heaven upon the undertakers."[8] Even so, the trade continued. By the end of 1568, some sixty thousand Africans had been taken from Sierra Leone alone.

Initially the English plied their trade with the Spanish who required slaves for their Caribbean Islands. In the first half of the seventeenth century, however, England began ranging out, establishing an empire of her own in the West Indies. Barbados, St. Kitts, Antigua, Montserrat, and Jamaica came under her domain. The Bahamas were likewise part of the growing, powerful New World colonial system. Additional slaves, in increasing numbers, were required for plantations producing sugar and cotton, as well as for work in military fortifications.

In 1618 James I chartered the Company of the Adventurers of London to trade in parts of Africa. This business organization built the first trading post in West Africa, a venture that proved to be a financial failure. For a time the Dutch provided the English with slaves. Another attempt was made in 1631 when Charles I gave a company of traders a thirty-one-year monopoly on the trade in Guinea, Benin, and Angola. By the middle of the seventeenth century the growing sugar industry in Barbados prompted Charles II to charter the Royal African Company to deliver three thousand Negroes annually to the British West Indies. Terms such as "black ivory" and "black gold" came into use as the traffic in human flesh became increasingly remunerative and "middle passage" increasingly horrible. Daniel Defoe's *The Life and Strange, Surprising Adventures of Robinson Crusoe* of 1719 portrays a Puritan view of slavery, and the setting, traditionally, was Tobago!

By the beginning of the eighteenth century, Britain—now the expanding influence in Europe, far outranking Spain and Portugal—virtually had a monopoly on the slave trade. Thanks to the Asiento clauses of the Treaty of Utrecht, 1713, Spain and France were now deprived of their valuable slave trade. Superseding

Holland, another Protestant power, Britain was coming into her own, replacing the Roman Catholic nations in domination of trade in West Africa slaves. This had been clearly seen in the latter part of the seventeenth century. Between 1680 and 1686, 20,000 Blacks were imported annually into the British colonies in America and the West Indies. During the same period, 74,000 Blacks were transported by all nations. In the span of 1680–1786, 2,130,000 slaves were imported into British colonies; 60,000 were brought into Jamaica. They were bought for about £20-25 in West Africa and sold for £40-50 each in Jamaica.

Britannia indeed ruled not only the waves but also the slave trade. She was, of course, far from being alone in advancing the highly profitable sugar colonies, and slaves were essential components. "Between 60 and 70 percent of all the Africans who survived the voyages to the New World were destined for Europe's sugar colonies."[9] For the British planter especially, it was a golden age. Sugar prices were high, transportation costs low, and there was "an ample supply of labor."[10]

Tragically, the immeasurable Sudanese area of West Africa, where the great nations of Ghana, Mali, and Songhay had once been so powerful, was now a source of slaves. Cities, such as Timbuktu, once flourishing centers for the arts and sciences—as the great University of Sankore—had gone into decline. True, to the east and south the states "Mossi, Hausa, Kanem-Bornu and Ashanti retained their political identities down to the eighteenth and nineteenth centuries,"[11] but the areas touching the Atlantic, where great kings, Tenkamenin, Sundiata, Mansa Musa, and Aska had once ruled in splendor, were now ghastly slave forts, barracoons—combination military installations and temporary holding stockades for slaves brought from the interior, awaiting transfer to slave vessels. Some forty of these forts dotted the African coast from Senegal to the Bight of Benin. In 1791, Holland held fifteen such citadels, Britain had fourteen, Portugal and Denmark four each, and France three.[12]

The Conditions of Slavery

The slave excursion was made up of three passages: (1) the journey from the interior to the coast (sometimes a matter of a thousand miles), (2) the transportation by ship from the coast to market, known as "middle passage," and (3) the trip from market to the home port.

Horrors of middle passage became clear. Benezet cited the writings of a Captain Philips, whose Surgeon's Journal for December 29, 1724, recounted how Philips was advised to cut off the legs and arms of some slaves in order to terrify the rest into submission.[13] Other captains had employed this measure to prevent Africans from throwing themselves into the sea.

Again, Benezet quotes from John Atkins, a surgeon with Admiral Ogle's squadron, aboard the *Harding*. He told of a ship ready to sail for the West Indies from Guinea with some four or five hundred Africans. A fire broke out aboard ship and was shortly out of control, burning toward the powder kegs. The sailors attempted to remove the chain which bound the slaves, but the key could not be found. The ship exploded with a large portion of the slaves yet on board. Three Portuguese vessels were in sight, and they put lifeboats overboard. These took some two hundred fifty slaves from the water, still chained together, yet alive. Fifty of these died on shore "being mostly of those who were fettered together by iron shackles, which as they jumped into the sea, had broken their legs." The two hundred remaining "were soon disposed of, for account of the owners to other purchasers."[14]

Benezet told of the manner in which Africans were brought aboard slavers, a firsthand account, from John Barbot, of the French Company:

Their masters strip them of all they have on their backs, so that they come on board stark naked, as well women as men. In which condition they are obliged to continue, if the master of the ship is not so charitable (which he commonly is) as to bestow something on them to cover their nakedness. Six or seven hundred are sometimes put on board a vessel, where they lie as close together as its [sic] possible for them to be crowded.[15]

Life in the West Indies

Existence—it could hardly be known as life—in the Caribbean was little less wrenching than the passage. It was called "seasoning in the islands." Many slaves remained in the Caribbean, others were taken to the colonies in North America. Sir Hans Sloan's *Natural History of Jamaica* is Benezet's source for a slave's manner of subsisting from day to day.

The wearing them out with continual labour, before they have lived out half their days? The severe whipping and torturing them even to death, if they resist his insupportable tyranny. Let the hardiest slave-holder look forward to that tremendous day, when he must give an account to God of his stewardship.[16]

An illustration was given of a Negro man in his fifties, who had a wife and children in Guinea, his own country. When he went to get water for the children, he was violently seized and brought to Jamaica and sold. He married again and had two children by that wife. After some years he was separated from the second wife and their children when he was taken to South Carolina. Here he had a third wife, by whom he had another child. Again, he was disunited from wife and child, moved, and always remained a slave. Said Benezet:

Can any, whose mind is not rendered quite obdurate by the love of wealth, hear these relations, without being deeply touched with sympathy and sorrow; and doubtless the case of many, very many of these afflicted people, upon enquiry would be found to be attended with circumstances equally tragical and aggravating. . . . Does not justice loudly call for its being restored to them? Have they not the same right to demand it as any of us should have, if we had been violently snatched by Pyrates from our native land? Is it not the duty of every dispenser of justice, who is not forgetful of his own humanity, to remember, that these are men, and to be declared free?[17]

Scant wonder it is that the sugar produced during the eighteenth century in the West Indies was called "bitter sugar" by those who endured backbreaking toil in the cane fields.

By 1807, Liverpool shipping companies had one hundred eighty-five slave ships capable of transporting a total of forty thousand human victims. The familiar design of the hole of these vessels, with human cargo placed layer upon layer, prompted William Wilberforce's remark, "Never can so much misery be found condensed into so small a space as in a slave ship." Between the fifteenth and nineteenth centuries—a four-hundred-year period—it is estimated that a total of some fifteen million Africans were coerced and transported to the Americas.[18]

Slavery in North America

Blacks played a long and important, albeit unrecognized, role in North American history, life, and culture. Pedro Niño—very likely a black man—accompanied

Columbus, as one of his crew, on the 1492 voyage. Other Africans were with the Spanish conquistadores: Hernando de Alarcón, Coronado, Narváez. In 1526, Negro slaves in a Spanish colony—in what is now South Carolina—revolted, with success and fled to the Indians. In 1538 Estevanico, a noted black explorer known as Little Stephen, led an expedition from Mexico City, discovering, as the Spanish termed it, Arizona and New Mexico, and claiming these territories for Spain.[19] He may have gone as far north as Kansas, where he died.

The arrival, August 20, 1619—the traditional date— of the *Jesus* at Jameston, Virginia, with its company of twenty black indentured servants, marks the first Africans to come to the English colonies of North America. A contemporary wrote, "About the last of August came a Dutch man of warre that sold us 20 negars." These people were not slaves, but indentured servants who were to work for seven years to pay passage. Among the passengers were Antony and Isabella. (Their surname may have been Johnson, though Bennett says, "They had no surname.") Their son, William Tucker, named for a local planter, was born probably either January 1, 2, or 3, 1624, and is regarded to be the first African child born in the English colonies. This child was baptized in the Church of England, very likely, on January 3, 1624. An Anthony Johnson (possibly the same person as Antony) was an early arrival at Jamestown. Tradition says he became wealthy, and in turn owned slaves.

Black presence in the British colonies of North America was the prelude to slavery. Freedom was not extended to the slaves; even Christian baptism did not convey liberty. In 1641, Massachusetts became the first colony to give statutory recognition to slavery. This was followed in rapid succession by Connecticut in 1650, Virginia in 1661, Maryland in 1663, New York and New Jersey in 1664, South Carolina in 1682, Rhode Island and Pennsylvania in 1700. North Carolina in 1715,[20] and Georgia in 1750. Slavery was, ergo, part of the fabric of American life and culture.

The kindly, concerned Quakers of Germantown, Pennsylvania, in their monthly meeting, February 18, 1688, raised their protest against slavery.[21] It was a voice crying in the wilderness.

On the eve of the American Revolution, one third of the population of the colonies was not free: either slave or indentured servants, black and white. In 1775, by estimate, Negroes totaled one-fifth of the population which approximated 2,500,000. There were some free Blacks, but the number was small. Almost all black people were slaves. New England had 2.4 percent or approximately 15,800 Blacks. In the Middle Colonies, New York had an estimated 25,000, New Jersey 10,000, and Pennsylvania 6,000. The southern colonies had something less than half a million, perhaps 400,000 Blacks. In 1790 there were less than 700,000 slaves in the United States. By 1830 the number had grown to 2,000,000.[22]

CHAPTER

II

JOHN WESLEY AND HIS FAMILY

*T*he Wesleys were honest, tenacious, and godly. Their Wesley-Annesley tradition was one of simple living, deep personal piety, sound academic training, and bold prophetic utterances—utterances often as stubborn as they were fearless. An intense Puritan resolve had been inherited, along with a passionate concern for the oppressed, whoever or wherever the oppressed might be.

The Family

Bartholomew Westley was rector of Catherston and Charmouth in Dorset in 1650. His father was Herbert Westley, in the county of Devon. Perhaps there was high symbolism in the name given at baptism: Bartholomew, for on that feast day, Saint Bartholomew's Day, 1662, the good clergyman was ejected from his living. He was trained in both medicine and divinity, which was fortunate, because after he was thrust out of the parish he worked as a physician. His occasional preaching, his true livelihood, scarcely brought in enough to provide bare necessities. All the while, his stubborn pride prevented him from kowtowing to the hierarchy of the church.

John Westley was born in 1636 and received his initial training for the ministry from his father Bartholomew. John then went to New Inn Hall, Oxford, and took his M.A. degree. He was a specialist in oriental languages. In 1658, during Oliver Cromwell's Protectorate, John was made vicar of Winterborne, Whitchurch, in Dorset. Once more, on that Saint Bartholomew's Day of 1662, the second-generation Westley was evicted from his church, because he refused to use the Book of Common Prayer. He and his father and two thousand other self-willed ministers suffered a similar fate. They could have relented and stayed at their churches, but their consciences would not permit them to do so. John Westley and his family were forced to live in poverty; John was even confined in prison at Poole. He died in 1678, a faithful servant of the Christ "whom he had served with his whole heart, according to the best light he had."

Samuel Wesley,[1] who altered the spelling of the name, was born in 1666. He went to Oxford in 1683 and became a servitor at Exeter College. This means he worked his way (his father certainly would have possessed scant funds to assist), serving other students and suffering the taunts of snobbish, wealthy aristocrats. He graduated with the M.A. degree and was ordained priest by the Bishop of London on February 24, 1689 (having departed from the Puritan tradition of his father and grandfather). He eventually became rector of Epworth in 1697. Here he and his highly talented, high-spirited wife, and their ever-increasing brood of children did the best they could to make ends meet. His obstinate courage would not permit him to leave his unhappy parish, where he was almost constantly opposed by his resentful parishioners (who maimed his cattle and set fire to his house). There was a highly prophetic side to Samuel. He once contemplated going to Africa as a missionary. He rejoiced in the prison reforms of James Edward Oglethorpe, and well he might, since he had been incarcerated for debt. On July 6, 1734, Samuel wrote General Oglethorpe, complimenting him on his plans to establish a new colony, Georgia, as a refuge for those languishing in English debtors' prisons. "May I be admitted, while such crowds of our nobility and gentry are pouring in their congratulations, to press with my poor mite of thanks into the presence of one who so well deserves the title of UNIVERSAL BENEFACTOR OF MAN-KIND?"[2] Samuel died at Epworth on April 25, 1735, and was buried in the yard of the church he served for thirty-nine years.

Susanna Annesley was born in London on January 20, 1669, the twenty-fifth child of the noted Dr. Samuel Annesley, known as the Saint Paul of Nonconformity. A woman of beauty, intellect, and great piety, she had the courage to leave the Puritan tradition of her illustrious father and become a High Church Anglican. She married Samuel Wesley in 1688; nineteen children were born to the union, ten surviving infancy. Under her direction the children were well trained, as well educated as any in England. Rigorous discipline was combined with methodical study and a well-organized devotional life. Her ties with son John were unusually strong. Her comment as John and Charles sailed for Georgia, "Had I twenty sons, I should rejoice that they were all so employed, though I should never see them more."[3] She died on July 30, 1742, requesting, "Children, as soon as I am released, sing a psalm of praise to God."[4] Her legacy of resolute, organized piety, and desire to extend the gospel message would have far-reaching consequences.

John Wesley was born June 17, 1703, at Epworth. Reared under Susanna's watchful eye and Samuel's scholarly preaching, John became a foundation scholar at Charterhouse School in London on January 28, 1714. He entered Christ Church, Oxford, on January 24, 1720. His older brother Samuel, Jr., had preceded him, and his younger brother Charles would follow. During his student years John corresponded with his parents. In 1725 he decided to assume holy orders. He also began a rigorous study of "practical divinity," including the reading of *Imitation of Christ* by à Kempis (and Groote), as well as Jeremy Taylor's *Holy Living and Dying,* William Law's *Serious Call to a Devout and Holy Life,* and Henry Scougal's *Life of God in the Soul of Man.* Wesley was ordained deacon at Oxford in 1725; he took his M.A. on February 14, 1727; he was ordained as priest in 1728. He served for a time as his father's curate, but in his role as a Fellow of Lincoln he pursued the life of scholar and tutor.

It was during the years at Oxford that a small group of students met to discuss matters of faith. Usually called the Holy Club, the company provided spiritual insight and proved to be of enormous benefit to John Wesley.[5] Many life patterns were here established. Not only was there intense soul-searching, the quest for holiness, but there was also a vital realization of social need. They visited the poor, with substantial contributions from Wesley's stipend as an Oxford don, and they established regular visits to the prison.

Oxford days were concluded when John had an opportunity to go to Georgia as chaplain to the colony and missionary to the Indians. "Our end in leaving our native country was not to avoid want, God having given us plenty of temporal blessings, nor to gain riches or honour, . . . but singly this—to save our souls, to live wholly to the glory of God."[6]

Charles Wesley was born December 18, 1707. He, like others in the family, was first educated at home. He then entered Westminster School in London in 1716. In 1726 he became a student at Christ Church, Oxford. He was a leader in the ardent, methodical study cluster, questing for holy living. In 1735, in preparation for a ministry in Georgia, Charles was ordained a priest in the Church of England.

Call to Ministry in America

Thus the two brothers, ably qualified with their University of Oxford degrees and Anglican holy orders, prepared for missionary work in a frontier colony. In a strange, might it be called providential, way the Wesleys were about to have their foremost encounter with the realities of slavery. Blacks were about to become part of their existential experience.[7]

CHAPTER
III

GEORGIA:
THE WESLEYS MEET SLAVERY

*P*eople were living on the coast of what is now Georgia as early as 6000 to 5000 B.C. During the Woodland Period—1000 B.C. to A.D. 700–900—additional people were in the Georgia area. Centuries later, Indian tribes—language groupings really, Cherokee, Creek, Guale, Yamacraw, and Yamasee—lived in the territory. Georgia belonged to them long before any Europeans appeared on the scene.

Hernando de Soto passed through the region in 1540 as he ruthlessly made his way toward the Mississippi. "In quest of Indians, a hundred men and women were taken. They were led off in chains, with collars about the neck, to carry luggage and grind corn, doing labor proper to servants."[1]

French Huguenots, under Jean Ribault, reached the mouth of the St. Johns River, but the Spanish would not tolerate their presence. In 1566, to drive away these French Protestants, Pedro Menéndez de Avilés built a fort on St. Catherines Island, the first Spanish settlement in Georgia, a territory Spain called "Guale."

England entered the scene in 1663 when Charles II granted the area to the Lords Proprietors of Carolina.

It was not until 1721, that Fort King George was erected, near the mouth of the Altamaha. It was abandoned in 1727.

A Royal Charter was granted in 1732 to the youngest of the thirteen colonies and appropriately named for George II, "a separate province, distinct from South Carolina . . . under the name of Georgia."[2]

Blacks played no small role in the formation of Georgia. In 1730 a party of London philanthropists did some serious thinking about a bequest of £1,000 which had been placed in trust for the grand and noble purpose of converting Negroes. This legacy became a factor in Georgia plans.[3] In addition to Oglethorpe's dream of helping those in debtor's prison, freedom would be given to all. The Charter declared: "All and every person or persons who shall at any time hereafter inhabit or reside within our said province, shall be and are hereby declared to be free, and shall not be subject to or bound to obey any laws, orders, statutes or constitutions which have been heretofore made, ordered and enacted." There was more, "All and every the persons which shall happen to be born within the said province, and every of their children and posterity, shall have and enjoy all liberties, franchises and immunities of free denizions and natural born subjects."[4]

These noble regulations, it seems, did not apply to *all*. Shortly, "His Majesty thought fit to pass some laws since the Charter, whereby the Inhabitants are restrained from the use of Negroes, from the use of Rum, and from Trading with the Indians without Lycence."[5] There soon followed "An Act for rendering the Colony of Georgia more defensible by Prohibiting the Importation and use of Black Slaves or Negroes into the same." It was assumed the Georgia colonists "could ill afford the purchase"[6] of Africans. White indentured servants "did not appear to offer the disadvantages" that were imagined attendant upon the use of slaves.

This Eden, "The Most Delightful Country of the Universe," thus prohibited slavery, not on moral, but economic grounds. The "Persons sent from *England* on the Charity were of the Unfortunate" and these folk, heavily in debt, would have a second chance. They would be English people, not Africans. When Oglethorpe first arrived in Georgia, on February 12, 1733, only about a dozen or so of the 120 settlers aboard the *Anne* were debtors, and few if any of them were rabble. They were, for the most part, people of business and artisans who, unfortunately, had fallen on hard times.

The first Blacks appearing in Georgia, very likely, came from South Carolina as workers. "Col. Bull brought with him 4 of his Negroes who were Sawyers, to assist the Colony; and also, brought provisions for them, being resolved to put the Trust to no expense."[7] Other Blacks probably came, either in flight from South Carolina (where slavery flourished) or they were brought covertly as slaves, public notice carefully avoided.

Enter the Wesleys

It was Dr. John Burton of Corpus Christi, Oxford, a Trustee for Georgia and a Patron of the Society for the Propagation of the Gospel, who wrote John Wesley on September 8, 1735, "Your short conference with Mr. Oglethorpe has raised the hopes of many good persons that you and yours would join in an undertaking which cannot be better executed than by such instruments."[8]

Burton wrote another long letter to Wesley on September 28, 1735, from Eton College:

One end for which we were associated was the conversion of negro slaves. As yet nothing has been attempted in this way. But a door is opened, and not far from home. The Purrysburgers [in South Carolina] have purchased slaves; they act under our influence, and Mr. Oglethorpe will think it advisable to begin there. You see the harvest is truly great— καὶ τίς ἱκανός ἐστι πρὸς ταῦτα ["And who is sufficient for these things?"]; this is a point among others to be kept in view.[9]

It must be emphasized that slavery thrived in South Carolina. Georgia, as the Wesleys would come to know, did not permit it. The Wesleys vigorously applauded the original Georgia ban on slavery.

Wesley wrote an extended reply to Burton on October 10, 1735, insisting, "My chief motive, to which all the rest are subordinate, is the hope of saving my own soul. I hope to learn the true sense of the gospel of Christ by preaching it to the heathens . . . . From these, therefore, I hope to learn the purity of that faith which was once delivered to the saints, the genuine sense and full extent of those laws which none can understand who mind earthly things." He added, "But you will perhaps ask, Can't you save your own soul in England as well as in Georgia? I answer, No, neither can I hope to attain the same degree of holiness here which I may there."[10]

It was settled. Accompanying the Wesleys were Benjamin Ingham and Charles Delamotte. The Earl of Egmont perceived, "I take the sudden resolution of the four gentlemen now mentioned of going over to help the cause of religion as a particular providence and mark of God's favour to our designs."[11] All were convinced the mission was of God and had God's blessing.

The voyage began about 9:00 A.M. on Tuesday, October 14, 1735, on the *Simmonds*. The four Englishmen continued their strict Oxford schedule.

From four in the morning till five each of us used private prayer. From five to seven we read the Bible together, carefully comparing it (that we might not lean to our own understandings) with the writings of the earliest ages. At seven we breakfasted. At eight were the public prayers, at which were present usually between thirty or forty of our eighty passengers.[12]

The pace accelerated hour by hour throughout the day until finally, "Between nine and ten we went to bed, where neither the roaring of the sea nor the motion of the ship could take away the refreshing sleep which God gave us." It is remarkable, indeed, that this was to be their life-style in pioneer Georgia!

A series of frightful storms overtook the vessel, and John Wesley candidly delineated the state of his soul, his haunting fear of death, "I was unfit, for I was unwilling to die."[13] During this traumatic, extended turbulence he later acknowledged the spiritual power of the Moravians, some twenty of whom were aboard ship, "The Germans . . . calmly sang on." After inquiry, he was told, "No; our women and children are not afraid to die." The indelible impression made by these German pietists became increasingly evident throughout the Georgia experience.

Arrival

At last the protracted voyage ended. On Wednesday, February 4, 1736, "About noon the trees [of Georgia] were visible from the mast." On Friday, February 6, 1736, "About eight in the morning I first set my foot on American ground," recorded John Wesley. When the other passengers came ashore a prayer service was held, with Wesley reading from Mark 6. His comment about the arrival, "God grant that, through patience and comfort of His Holy Word, we may ever hold fast the blessed hope of our calling!"[14]

The Wesleys were now in a frontier milieu, which explains many of the blunders. No longer was there the support of the Epworth household. Letters were exchanged, but the Atlantic now separated the family. There was no Holy Club—albeit Burton's suggestion to transfer it in toto to Georgia. Stability and comfort of the University of Oxford no longer existed. Likewise there were no refreshing, delightful visits to the Kirkham rectory at Stanton—home of that stimulating company of witty, charming young people. The Wesley brothers confronted an altogether new environment. They would learn much.

Charles

Charles Wesley, "Secretary for Indian Affairs" and also secretary to General Oglethorpe, had a doleful ministry lasting only five months. On Tuesday, March 9, 1736, "about three in the afternoon, I first set foot on St. Simon's Island,"[15] he noted. He worked diligently to fulfill his responsibilities both ministerial and secretarial. He was gullible; he failed to understand some designing women who had come on the *Simmonds*. He was, thanks to gossip, soon at cross purposes with the General.

Brother John was hastily summoned from Savannah to bring peace to an unhappy situation, but to no avail. It was not because Charles did not try; he seemed to trip over his own feet. Nonetheless, he clearly demonstrated a deep concern for people. He attempted to befriend a serving girl, and the result was a humiliating scene: "While I was talking in the street with poor Catherine, her mistress came up to us, and fell upon me with the utmost bitterness and scurrility." He went on melancholically, she "said she would blow me up, and my brother, . . . she would be revenged, and expose my d--d hypocrisy, my prayers four times a day by beat of drum, and abundance more," at which point it is almost possible to see the downcast Charles take a long breath and continue, "which I cannot write, and thought no woman, though taken from Drurylane, could have spoken."[16]

It was July 21 when Charles learned the happy news that he was to return to England. Oglethorpe's parting advice, "I should recommend to you marriage, rather than celibacy." Charles read the lesson for July 26, "Arise, let us go hence," and noted, "Accordingly at twelve I took my final leave of Savannah. When the boat put off I was surprised that I felt no more joy in leaving such a place of sorrows."[17]

Slavery: A Revelation

John accompanied his brother to Charleston the latter part of July, 1736. This was the first visit by either to this city and to the Colony of South Carolina. Here the brothers saw the brutal realism of slavery. Of course they had read much on the subject, and they would have seen Africans in England, but now it all came home to them. One situation, possibly a scene, especially struck Charles; he would never forget the event or the lesson which he learned. In his private *Journal* he made a full entry. When the *Journal* was published, posthumously, the following appeared, dated Monday, August 2:

I had observed much, and heard more, of the cruelty of masters towards their negroes; but now I received an authentic account of some horrid instances thereof. The giving a child a slave of its own age to tyrannize over, to beat and abuse out of sport, was, I myself saw, a common practice.[18]

Charles did not stop here. He had a great deal more to say about slavery. The account is of major significance.

> Nor is it strange, being thus trained up in cruelty, they should afterwards arrive at so great perfection in it; that Mr. Star, a gentleman I often met at Mr. Lasserre's, should, as he himself informed L[asserre], first nail up a negro by the ears, then order him to be whipped in the severest manner, and then to have scalding water thrown over him, so that the poor creature could not stir for four months after. Another much-applauded punishment is, drawing their slaves' teeth. One Colonel Lynch is universally known to have cut off a poor negro's legs; and to kill several of them every year by his barbarities.
>
> It were endless to recount all the shocking instances of diabolical cruelty which these men (as they call themselves) daily practice upon their fellow-creatures; and that on the most trivial occasions. I shall only mention one more, related to me by a Swiss gentleman, Mr. Zouberbuhler, an eye-witness, of Mr. Hill, a dancing-master in Charlestown. He whipped a she-slave so long, that she fell down at his feet for dead. When, by the help of a physician, she was so far recovered as to show signs of life, he repeated the whipping with equal rigour, and concluded with dropping hot sealing-wax upon her flesh. Her crime was overfilling a tea-cup.

Charles concluded:

> These horrid cruelties are the less to be wondered at, because the government itself, in effect, countenances and allows them to kill their slaves, by the ridiculous penalty appointed for it, of about seven pounds sterling, half of which is usually saved by the criminal's informing against himself. This I can look upon as no other than a public act to indemnify murder.[19]

This macabre entry in Charles Wesley's *Journal* is among the first, if not the first, documents which would become evidence in the thought processes of the Wesley brothers as they formed their opposition to the brutal institution of slavery. Charles Wesley had written it, and doubtless discussed it with his brother. It was the utter inhumanity of it all which Charles could not expunge from his memory. The dehumanizing of it, as in the idea that one child might own another child, as a pet, to be treated as a kitten or puppy—gentle and loving one moment, angry and abusive another. The sheer sadism toward a human being—inflicted by a human being. It was beyond Charles' comprehension, yet he knew it was taking place. Such cruel, demeaning treatment by one person toward another was a fact. This was, possibly, the initial encounter with slavery by the brothers. They saw it in all its savage realism.

As the years passed, as the Wesleys became old men, it is interesting to speculate: Did they reminisce about Georgia? Did they discuss the visit to Charleston, recalling the slave scenes they had witnessed, and the testimonies of the pitiless treatment of Africans?

Charles' Homecoming

Charles Wesley was only too glad to leave America, but he was not running away. He was, among other things, ill. In Boston he had to be assisted aboard ship to return to England. Once back in Britain, he made a forthright report to the Trustees concerning his brother's ministry in Georgia:

That when he arrived at Savannah he found the people had been miserably neglected by our late minister, Mr. Quincey; that but three persons partook of the communion, and the people diverted themselves with shooting on Sundays; but before he came away his brother, who is minister now there, had forty communicants every Sunday and on great holy days; that he preaches by heart and has a full assembly; that prayers are said twice every day, in the morning and at night, by reason the day is spent at labour in the fields.[20]

Oglethorpe returned to England and met Charles on Tuesday, February 15, 1737. Charles said of the meeting, "I told Mr. Oglethorpe of my desire of returning with him to Georgia . . . as a Clergyman; but as to my Secretary's place, I begged . . . where, when, and how I should resign it."[21]

Charles Wesley was hardly the failure in Georgia that most people assume. He had courage. His confrontation with the horrors of slavery enabled him to have a new understanding of the monstrous business. Seeds were planted in his mind and imagination.

Years later the Sweet Singer of Methodism composed a poem, which appeared in 1758 and 1781, entitled:

For the Heathens

Lord over all, if thou hast made,
  Hast ransomed every soul of man,
Why is the grace so long delayed,
  Why unfulfilled the saving plan?
The bliss for Adam's race designed,
  When will it reach to all mankind?

Art thou the God of Jews alone,
  And not the God of Gentiles too?
To Gentiles make thy goodness known,
  Thy judgments to the nations show;
Awake them by the gospel call—
Light of the world, illumine all!

The servile progeny of Ham
  Seize as the purchase of thy blood;
Let all the heathens know thy name;
  From idols to the living God
The dark Americans convert,
And shine in every pagan heart!

As lightning lanced from East to West
  The coming of thy kingdom be;
To thee, by angel hosts confessed,
  Bow every soul and every knee;
Thy glory let all flesh behold,
And then fill up thy heavenly fold.[22]

John Wesley Meets Black People

John Wesley's service in Georgia lasted some twenty-two months. It was a difficult time. His frustrations, his sense of failure, his disappointment in love, his numerous personal controversies all added up to an experience like unto his father's ministry at Epworth. As in the circumstance of Samuel Wesley, it was true of John: the ministry was far from failure. Not the least aspect of which was his introduction to Africans. This took place in South Carolina.

On Saturday, July 31, 1736, John Wesley made the entry, "We came to Charlestown." He had accompanied Charles thus far. The Reverend Alexander Garden, the Bishop of London's Commissary for South Carolina, invited Wesley to preach on Sunday the first of August. "About three hundred were present at the morning service . . . about fifty at the Holy Communion." Wesley then made a special notation: "I was glad to see several negroes at church, one of whom told me she was there constantly, and that her old mistress (now dead) had many times instructed her in the Christian religion." This seems to have been the opportunity Wesley wanted: the chance to discuss spiritual matters. He was obviously delighted to be able to engage the woman in further conversation.

I asked her what religion was. She said she could not tell. I asked if she knew what a soul was. She answered, 'No.' I said, 'Do not you know there is something in you different from your body? Something you cannot see or feel?' She replied, 'I never heard so much before.' I added, 'Do you think, then, a man dies altogether as a horse dies?' She said, 'Yes, to be sure.'

Wesley was surprised and bewildered, "O God, where are Thy tender mercies? Are they not over all Thy works? When shall the Sun of Righteousness arise on these outcasts of men, with healing in His wings!"[23] It was a conversational pattern he would repeat.

Monday, August 2, found a busy Wesley rushing back to Georgia. He was exceedingly disappointed that he was unable to visit Alexander Skene, on whose plantation there were "about fifty Christian negroes."[24]

Back at his post in Georgia, Wesley was continually on the move. Friday, August 20, 1736, was a tiring day. He rose at 4:45 A.M. and in the course of the long day, at 9:00 A.M., was at home transcribing George Herbert. When this was completed he turned to *The Negro's Advocate*, and spent two hours reading it. This was probably Morgan Godwyn's *The Negro's and Indian's Advocate, suing for their Admission into the Church*, published in London, 1680. A twelve-page *Supplement* was published the following year.[25]

Wesley made a second visit to South Carolina, for the meeting of Anglican clergymen. He narrated the events, beginning Friday, April 15, 1737. "I walked over to Ashley Ferry, twelve miles from Charlestown, and thence, in the afternoon, went to Mr. Guy, the minister of Ashley, and to Colonel Bull's seat, two miles further." The Colonel's residence charmed Wesley; he said it was "the pleasantest place I have yet seen in America," with a wide assortment of trees and plants "which are esteemed in England, but which the laziness of the Americans seldom suffers them to raise."[26]

Wesley was with Alexander Garden on another Sunday. Garden invited Wesley to preach, and "I did so, on these words of the Epistle for the day: 'Whatsoever is born of God overcometh the world, and this is the victory which overcometh the world, even our faith.' " Wesley afterward sent the sermon to Garden, to whom he was "indebted for many kind and generous offices."[27]

It had been Wesley's intention to return to Georgia following the service, but "stormy and contrary winds" forced his vessel back to Charleston. There, at Mr. Garden's he met "the clergy of South Carolina" who had come for the "annual Visitation."[28] This gave Wesley an opportunity to hobnob with his fellow Anglican clerics.

While in South Carolina, on Saturday, April 23, Wesley talked with Mr. Thompson, minister of St. Bartholomew's, near Ponpon. Said Wesley, "My being disappointed of a passage home by water, he offered me one of his horses if I would go by land, which I gladly accepted of." Wesley continued, saying Thompson "went with me twenty miles, and sent his servant [probably a slave] to guide me the other twenty to his house."[29]

It was at the Reverend Mr. Thompson's residence in South Carolina that John Wesley engaged in a protracted conversation with a black woman. Her name was Nanny. This major piece of dialogue, which Wesley regarded important enough to record in its entirety, may be the first lengthy, in-depth conversation he ever had with a black person. Some of his questions were repeats of those he used in the earlier meeting with the woman at Garden's church.

Finding a young negro there, who seemed more sensible than the rest, I asked her how long she had been in Carolina. She said two or three years; but that she was born in Barbados, and had lived there in a minister's family from a child.

Wesley was obviously intrigued. He plied her with questions, probably pounding the table, gently, as he pursued the conversation.

I asked her whether she went to church there. She said, 'Yes, every Sunday, to carry my mistress's children.' I asked her what she had learned at church. She said, 'Nothing; I heard a great deal, but did not understand it.' 'But what did your master teach you at home?' 'Nothing.' 'Nor your mistress?' 'No.'

Amazed that a person living in a clergyman's household would have learned nothing of the things of God,

Wesley decided to employ a different tactic. He began with, in his view, basic questions. "I asked, 'But don't you know that your hands and feet, and this you call your body, will turn to dust in a little time?' She answered, 'Yes.' "

Wesley continued, probing earnestly, reflecting his eighteenth-century theological background.

'But there is something in you that will not turn to dust, and this is what they call your soul. Indeed, you cannot see your soul, though it is within you; as you cannot see the wind, though it is all about you. But if you had not soul in you, you could no more see, or hear, or feel, than this table can. What do you think will become of your soul when your body turns to dust?' 'I don't know.'

Wesley, the emerging, if not stumbling, evangelist, now drove his point home, responding to the honest, straightforward statements of a sincere black woman. (Perchance there was more pounding of the table from time to time.)

'Why, it will go out of your body, and go up there, above the sky, and live always. God lives there. Do you know who God is?' 'No.' 'You cannot see Him, anymore than you can see your own soul. It is He that made you and me, and all men and women, and all beasts and birds, and all the world. It is He that makes the sun shine, and rain fall, and corn and fruits to grow out of the ground. He makes all these for us. But why do you think He made us? What did He make you and me for?' 'I can't tell.' 'He made you to live with Himself above the sky. And so you will, in a little time, if you are good. If you are good, when your body dies your soul will go up, and want nothing, and have whatever you desire. No one will beat or hurt you there. You will never be sick. You will never be sorry any more, nor afraid of anything. I can't tell you, I don't know how happy you will be; for you will be with God.'

Wesley concluded with his personal observation. It had been a penetrating dialogue, and doubtless exhausting for him, and certainly for Nanny. "The attention with which this poor creature listened to instruction is inexpressible. The next day she remembered all, readily answering every question; and said she would ask Him that made her to show her how to be good."[30]

This conversation is perhaps one of the most important Wesley had during his American ministry. It is valuable in that it reveals far more about Wesley than Nanny. The exchange of questions and answers must be taken at face value. It all comes from the first half of the eighteenth century. It is an honest interchange between two authentic people. A warning needs to be sounded: persons should not attempt to read into Wesley something that is not there. Words and ideas originating in late twentieth-century psychology, sociology, or anthropology do not belong.

A question can be raised, Why did Wesley not speak of the slave conditions under which Nanny was compelled to live? Was John Wesley, like Paul, essentially condoning slavery? Was his parlance chiefly an other worldly religion? After all, he spoke only of liberating her soul; no questions were asked about manumission of the physical.

A possible answer may be simply that Wesley was gauging his inquiries by the single measuring rod of spiritual reality, which may have been the woman's greatest need. On the other hand, this conversation may best illustrate the growing, learning experience that America proved to be for Wesley. John Wesley learned, thanks to Nanny. Obviously, he did not forget.

The following day, Sunday April 24, Wesley preached at the Ponpon Chapel. The next day, Thompson "sent his servant with me to Mr. Belinger's."[31] Doubtless, the servant was black. In this South Carolina visit, Wesley had the opportunity to be with Africans, to ride with them, to talk with them. Since slavery was forbidden in Georgia, he had few opportunities for conversation with Blacks. Long rides through South Carolina countryside and areas dense with palmetto and pine thickets would have afforded an ideal setting for free exchange, especially since the slave owner was not at hand with open ear and eye. Wesley was acquiring a great deal of information.

William Bellinger, at Ashepoo Ferry, entered the scene on Tuesday of that week. Riding in hard rain, the party reached Hugh Brian's[32] at three and dined. Wesley was patently impressed by Brian's kind treatment of his slaves and mentioned him thirty-seven years later in *Thoughts upon Slavery*. Brian went with Bellinger and Wesley to Mr. Palmer's "five miles short of his own plantation at Chulifinny." On Wednesday Wesley "came to Mr. Belinger's plantation, where the rain kept me till Friday." It was fortunate, because "Here I met [an old negro who was tolerably well instructed in the principles of Christianity, and who, as well as his fellow negroes and] a half Indian [woman] (one that had an Indian mother and a Spanish father) seemed earnestly desirous of further instruction." Wesley was enthralled. "One of them said, 'When I lived at Ashley Ferry, I could go to church every Sunday, but here we are buried in the woods. Though if there was any church within five or six miles, I am so lame I cannot walk, but I would crawl thither.' "[33]

Bellinger then sent a "negro lad" with Wesley, to conduct him to Purrysburg. Alas, it was a community "with no form or comeliness" and said to be the first settlement in South Carolina to introduce slavery. Wesley detested the place. "O earth! how long wilt thou hide blood? . . . cover thy slain?" This same black youth who had accompanied Wesley was "both very desirous and very capable of instruction." Wesley had an idea:

perhaps one of the easiest and shortest ways to instruct the American negroes in Christianity would be, first, to inquire after and find out some of the most serious of the planters. Then, having inquired of them which of their slaves were best inclined and understood English, to go to them from plantation to plantation, staying as long as appeared necessary to each.[34]

A few planters were interested. Wesley had earlier seen a letter from the Bishop of London "for Negro's Book on Confirmation."

Wesley took a boat, and on Saturday, April 30, returned to Savannah. The remaining nine months in Georgia were unusually hectic. He did not have an opportunity to make another plantation tour of South Carolina. It is unfortunate that he could not renew the several associations he had made with black folk. He certainly did not forget them.

Friday, December 2, 1737, was a sad day indeed. Wrote Wesley:

I saw clearly the hour was come for [me to fly for my life,] leaving this place; and as soon as evening prayers were over, about eight o'clock, the tide then serving, I shook off the dust of my feet, and left Georgia, after having preached the gospel there [with much weakness indeed and many infirmities,] not as I ought, but as I was able, one year and nearly nine months.[35]

Wesley made a third call in South Carolina. It was his longest visit to the city of Charleston. He took time to visit the dying Samuel Eveleigh.[36]

John Wesley was leaving America; he would never return. As he began sailing back to England, aboard the *Samuel*, on Monday, December 26, 1737, he recorded, "I began instructing a negro lad in the principles of Christianity."[37] It is very interesting that a black person became the one Wesley associated with in an hour of great personal need. Soon "another Negro" joined them.

Back in England, in January of 1738, Wesley reviewed the whole Georgia experience.

It is now two years and almost four months since I left my native country, in order to teach the Georgia Indians the nature of Christianity. But what have I learned myself in the meantime? Why, what I the least of all suspected, that I, who went to America to convert others, was never myself converted to God.[38]

The revealing question is, "But what have I learned myself?" Among other things, he had learned about slavery—what it was, what suffering was. He had gone primarily to convert the Indians. In reality he was able to achieve more for the black people. "A few steps have been taken towards publishing the glad tidings both to the African and American heathen."[39] Georgia and South Carolina had no small role in John Wesley's growth, understanding, and vision. As the years advanced, the nexus between Georgia and the Wesleys became increasingly evident. The colony had provided a particular environment for maturation—emotional, spiritual, and social. Both brothers began to acquire a new understanding of people—empathy—which in turn helped them see themselves. The two Oxonians had seen and heard of a very real world. Especially had their eyes been opened to the horrors of "that execrable villany"—the slave trade. Years later, when John Wesley wrote to Granville Sharp, October 11, 1787, he stated, "Ever since I heard of it first I felt a perfect detestation of the horrid Slave Trade."[40] This initial encounter would have been while in Georgia and South Carolina.

Disappointment from Georgia

One reason why John Wesley remained so concerned about black people in Georgia was that the idealistic words of the colony's charter were soon to be altered. Alas, by 1738 the Georgia colonists were petitioning the trustees for a free title to land and the use of slaves. One hundred and twenty-eight freemen signed the petition, making a point that there should not be unlimited use of African people, but a proportionate number to each white man, and to the quality of the land.[41] By 1740 there were Blacks in Georgia. "What few . . . had entered Georgia, chiefly with their masters from South Carolina, were soon banished according to the terms of the Negro Act, which Georgia constables were charged with executing."[42] Moreover, "Negroes were not even allowed to peddle wares along the waterfront at Savannah."[43]

John Wesley wrote to Anthony Benezet (at a much later date, 1774).

Mr. Oglethorpe you know went so far as to begin settling a colony without negroes, but at length the voice of those villains prevailed who sell their country and their God for gold, who laugh at human nature and compassion, and defy all religion, but that of getting money. It is certainly our duty to do all in our power to check this growing evil, and something may be done by spreading those tracts which place it in a true light. But I fear it will not be stopped till all the kingdoms of the earth become the kingdoms of our God.[44]

George Whitefield

Sad to relate, one who contributed so much to the Wesleyan Revival, George Whitefield, also played a part in Georgia slavery. Of Wesley's ministry in Georgia, Whitefield had glowing observations: "The good, Mr. John Wesley had done in America, under God, is inexpressible. His name is very precious among the people; and he has laid such a foundation, that I hope neither men nor devils will be able to shake."[45]

Early in his ministry, in 1740, Whitefield wote *A Letter to the Inhabitants of Maryland, Virginia, North and South Carolina,* berating them for their treatment of slaves. "I think God has a quarrel with you." Unhappily, a year later the great evangelist was advocating, "As for manuring more Land than the hired Servants and great Boys can manage, I think it is impracticable without a few Negroes." Before slaveholding became legal in Georgia, Whitefield purchased slaves to work at Bethesda Orphanage.[46]

Whitefield was a child of his time, and he must be seen in that light. If the slaves were treated kindly and were given the Christian gospel, Whitefield, and many eighteenth-century professing Christians (what of Jonathan Edwards?) saw nothing incongruous in the institution. John Wesley took an altogether different view. Among the eighteenth-century clergy, John Wesley was a man far ahead of his time. A social conscience was part of the fabric of the life of faith: this was Wesley.[47]

CHAPTER
IV

THE WESLEYS IN ENGLAND:
1738–1757

*T*he year 1738 proved to be the turning point for both of the Wesley brothers. It was a time of painful reflection on the Georgia experiment; there was that haunting sense of failure. It was likewise a disconcerting period of soul-searching, wherein both were greatly helped by friends and associates, not the least of which was the Moravian, Peter Böhler.

May of 1738 was pivotal. It was the month wherein the Wesleys experienced profound altering of direction and outlook.[1] Self-centeredness was replaced by an overwhelming concern that the gospel of Jesus Christ be shared with all of humankind. How did it come about?

Charles' Spiritual Birthday

On Whitsunday, May 21, 1738, Charles had a painful attack of pleurisy. Mr. Bray, a brazier "who knows nothing but Christ; yet by knowing him, knows and discerns all things," provided a room for Charles above his shop, Number 12 in Little Britain, London. Mrs. Turner, Bray's sister, was looking after the household.

That godly woman felt constrained by a vivid dream to say something to Charles, but was reluctant to witness to a clergyman. Her brother told her, "Speak you the words: Christ will do the work." She climbed the stair and announced, "In the name of Jesus of Nazareth, arise, and believe, and thou shalt be healed of all thy infirmities." Charles thought it was Mrs. Musgrave speaking, only to be told Mrs. Musgrave was not there. His heart was pounding, yet he feared to say, "I believe, I believe!"

Mrs. Turner returned to Charles' door and explained, "It was I, a weak, sinful creature, spoke; but the words were Christ's: he commanded me to say them, and so constrained me that I could not forbear." She told Charles what had taken place. "At the same time she was enlarged in love and prayer for all mankind, and commanded to go and assure me from Christ of my recovery, soul and body." Charles turned to Isaiah 40:1. Said he:

I now found myself at peace with God, and rejoiced in hope of loving Christ. My temper for the rest of the day was, mistrust of my own great, but before unknown, weakness. I saw that by faith I stood; by the continual support of faith, which kept me from falling, though of myself I am ever sinking into sin. I went to bed still sensible of my own weakness, (I humbly hope to be more and more so,) yet confident of Christ's protection.

The next morning, May 22, Charles awakened and rejoiced as he read Psalm 107. Wednesday evening, about 10 o'clock, brother John with a troop of friends came, saying, "I believe."[2] They joined in singing the "conversion hymn":

> Where shall my wond'ring soul begin?
> How shall I all to heaven aspire?

> A slave redeemed from death and sin,
> A brand plucked from eternal fire,
> How shall I equal triumphs raise,
> Or sing my great Deliverer's praise?[3]

Later, Charles wished:

> O for a thousand tongues to sing
> My dear Redeemer's praise!
> The glories of my God and King,
> The triumphs of his grace![4]

He had, indeed, given himself "up to Christ."

John's Heartwarming Experience

John Wesley carefully outlined his spiritual quest in his *Journal*, recounting events as early as age ten! "I had not sinned away that 'washing of the Holy Ghost.' " He continued, page after page. On May 24, 1738, at 5:00 A.M., he opened his Bible at random, as he frequently did, and chanced upon II Peter 1:4: "There are given unto us exceeding great and precious promises." Later he came upon Mark 12:34: "Thou art not far from the kingdom of God."

In the afternoon, probably Henry Purcell's rendition of Psalm 130 in the anthem "Out of the deep have I called unto thee, O Lord" at St. Paul's touched John Wesley and certainly spoke to his condition. Then, "In the evening I went very unwillingly to a society in Aldersgate Street." Very likely William Holland was reading:

Luther's preface to the *Epistle to the Romans*. About a quarter before nine, while he was describing the change which God works in the heart through faith in Christ, I felt my heart strangely warmed. I felt I did trust in Christ, Christ alone for salvation; and an assurance was given me that He had taken away *my* sins, even *mine,* and saved *me* from the law of sin and death.

It was John Wesley's liberating experience of the grace of God. It was not the end of probing questions, nor being "buffeted with temptations"[5] but rather, within a matter of months, a new Wesley was seen. He was preaching, traveling to Germany, turning to the fields. Never before in that well-ordered, carefully disciplined life had he known such freedom.

May 1738 had witnessed the spiritual rebirth of the Wesleys. There was a new zeal, not only for the things of God, but deep concerns for suffering humanity. It was the beginning of the Wesleyan Revival!

Charles, a Prison, a Black Man

Within two months after his encounter with the Holy Spirit on May 21, the Sweet Singer of Methodism was engaged in prison ministry—a manifestation of the nascent Revival. Charles Wesley records that on July 12, 1738, he was in London, preaching "at Newgate to the condemned felons, and visited one of them in his cell, sick of a fever; a poor black that had robbed his master." Charles went on, recounting:

I told him of one who came down from heaven to save lost sinners, and him in particular; described the sufferings of the Son of God, his sorrows, agony, and death. He listened with all the signs of eager astonishment; the tears trickled down his cheeks while he cried, "What! was it for me? Did God suffer all this for so poor a creature as me?" I left him waiting for the salvation of God.[6]

On Thursday, July 13, Charles was back at Newgate, praying, preaching, and administering the sacraments to the five condemned felons, exhorting "them with great comfort and confidence."

Charles returned on Friday and "spake strongly to the poor malefactors; and to the sick Negro in the condemned hole, moved by his sorrow and earnest desire of Christ Jesus." Saturday, "I preached there again with an enlarged heart; and rejoiced with my poor happy Black; who now *believes* the Son of God loved him, and gave himself for him."

Charles became quite ill on Sunday, but on Monday he was free from pain. He preached at Newgate. "At one I was with the Black in his cell . . . . Two more of the malefactors came. I had great help and power in prayer." Charles found himself overwhelmed, and the prisoners greatly moved. "The Black was quite happy."

On Tuesday, July 18, Charles was back at Newgate. "I administered the sacrament to the Black, and eight more; having first instructed them in the nature of it." He spent time, in the cells, talking with the condemned. At night he was locked in one of the cells; there was "mighty prayer" and all the criminals were present. They sang Samuel Wesley's hymn "Behold, the Saviour of mankind."

> Behold, the Saviour of mankind
> Nailed to the shameful tree;
> How vast the love that him inclined
> To bleed and die for thee![7]

Wednesday was the day of execution. "At six I prayed and sang with them all together." At half-past nine "their irons were knocked off, and their hands tied." Charles accompanied the condemned and described the grisly affair: "By half-hour past ten we came to Tyburn, waited till eleven: then were brought the children appointed to die. I got upon the cart . . . . We had prayed before that our Lord would show there was a power superior to the fear of death."

The prisoners were "all cheerful; full of comfort, peace, and triumph; assuredly persuaded Christ had died for them, and waited to receive them into paradise."

Charles went on: "The Black had spied me coming out of the coach, and saluted me with his looks. As often as his eyes met mine, he smiled with the most composed, delightful countenance I ever saw."

The entire company of condemned "expressed their desire of our following them to paradise. I never saw such calm triumph, such incredible indifference to dying." Again they sang "Behold, the Saviour of mankind" and "Faith in Christ" It was exactly "at twelve they were turned off." Charles spoke to the crowd, and then departed. "That hour under the gallows," said he, "was the most blessed hour of my life."[8]

Charles Wesley's account may read like maudlin sentimentality, but it was hardly that. The Revival was not mawkish pietism. Neither was this a chance vignette in the life of a busy clergyman. It was the Wesleyan Revival; in John Wesley's phrase, it was "Christianity in earnest."

Blacks and the Revival

John Wesley had not erased from his mind the black men and women whom he had met in South Carolina. In a brief notation in his diary, for Sunday, June 29, 1740, at 8:00 A.M. at Moorfields, Wesley "collected for the Negro school."[9] He failed to designate the school's name or location.

In 1743 John Wesley published his *Explanatory Notes upon the New Testament.* In his exposition of I Timothy 1:10, he describes: "*Man-stealers*—The worst of all thieves, in comparison of whom Highwaymen and House-breakers are innocent! What then are most Traders in Negroes, Procurers of Servants for *America,* and all who list Soldiers by Lies, Tricks, or Inticements."[10] The term "Man-stealers" became a choice phrase in Wesley's antislavery vocabulary. He made frequent use of it.

On Sunday, July 27, 1755, Wesley recorded, "I was much affected about this time by a letter sent from a gentleman in Virginia"—the Reverend Samuel Davies, an "able, zealous, and eloquent Presbyterian" of Hanover. Davies was later to become president of Princeton. His correspondence with Wesley is deeply touching. He wrote:

> The poor negro slaves here never heard of Jesus, or His religion, till they arrived at the land of their slavery in America, whom their masters generally neglect, as though immortality was not the privilege of their souls in common with their own. These poor Africans are the principal objects of my compassion, and, I think, the most proper subjects of your charity.

Davies went on to say the population of Virginia was "about three hundred thousand, and the one half of them are supposed to be negroes."[11] Wesley responded; books were sent.

The following year, March 1, 1756, Wesley made another reference to a letter from Davies. "When the books arrived I gave public notice after sermon," said Davies, "and desired such negroes as could read, and such white people as would make good use of them and were not able to buy, to come to my house." Of all the books sent by Wesley, none pleased the slaves more than "the Psalms and Hymns, which enable them to gratify their peculiar taste for psalmody.[12]

Another letter from Davies, written January 28, 1757, and noted by Wesley at the same date in his *Journal*, "My success is not equal to my wishes, . . . I have baptized near one hundred and fifty adult negroes of whom about sixty are communicants." Davies went on to say, "Among them in the first place, and then among the poor white people, I have distributed the books you sent me." He concluded, "And let me and my congregation, particularly my poor negro converts, be favoured with your prayers."[13]

Thus Wesley's Revival continued in England, Scotland, Wales, and Ireland, but its influence was not contained in the scepter'd isle alone. Books were going to Virginia. The beautiful Caribbean was about to be touched by the ministry of the man who "offered them Christ."

CHAPTER

V

WESLEYAN WITNESS
IN THE CARIBBEAN

*O*rganized Methodism first appeared in the West Indies, indeed in the Western Hemisphere, on the little island of Antigua in 1760,[1] possibly some six years prior to the Maryland/Virginia preaching of Robert Strawbridge, or the formation of the New York Society by Philip Embury and Barbara Heck or the Newfoundland/Nova Scotia work by Lawrence Coughlan and William Black. Methodist witness in the Caribbean dates from the activity of Nathaniel Gilbert, a descendant of the noted English navigator, Sir Humphrey Gilbert, half brother of Sir Walter Raleigh. Thomas Coke observed, "It was sometime in the year 1760 that Nathaniel Gilbert, Esq. . . . found himself in Antigua."[2]

Gilbert inherited a rich estate in Antigua and took up residence there. He was a man of rare skill: cultured, educated and with legal training. He was soon elected speaker of Antigua's Legislative Assembly. His brother Francis, of Kendal, England, had been converted in a Methodist meeting and became one of Wesley's preachers. He sent Nathaniel a number of Wesley's publications, including *The Appeals to Men of Reason and*

Religion.[3] This particular work completely altered Nathaniel's previously unfavorable opinion of Wesley. He wanted to meet the author, and that required a return to England. Gilbert had suffered poor health, so this called for a visit to his family home. Little did Nathaniel Gilbert realize what a change awaited him as he and his wife and their four daughters, together with at least three of his Negro house slaves, embarked for England.[4]

Meeting John Wesley

It was Tuesday, January 17, 1758, when Wesley made the entry in his *Journal*: "I preached at Wandsworth. A gentleman, come from America, has again opened a door in this desolate place. In the morning I preached at Mr. Gilbert's house. Two negro servants of his and a mulatto appear to be much awakened. Shall not His saving health be made known to all nations?"[5]

Wesley's preaching in Gilbert's home had telling effect, both on the household and on Wesley. Though not mentioned in his *Journal*, Wesley probably preached in the hearing of Gilbert's household a number of times. Eleven months after the initial visit, on Wednesday, November 29, 1758, Wesley made a joyful entry in his *Journal*. It was the culmination of that first preaching in the Gilbert home.

I rode to Wandsworth, and baptized two negroes belonging to Mr. Gilbert, a gentleman lately come from Antigua. One of these is deeply convinced of sin, the other rejoices in God her Saviour, and is the first African Christian I have known. But shall not our Lord, in due time, have these heathens also 'for His inheritance'?[6]

A momentous event it was! Wesley was obviously pleased beyond measure. It is a pity the names of the Africans are not here recorded. (The query cannot be avoided, Why did Wesley say "the first African Christian I have known"? Had he, at least for the moment, forgotten the people in South Carolina?)

Witness in Antigua

In due time the wealthy Mr. Gilbert and his household returned to Antigua where Gilbert began preaching, on the steps of his large plantation house (the same steps are still in existence; the house itself has been replaced). His several hundred slaves came to hear the gospel message. Nathaniel was joined by his brother Francis, who returned to Antigua, and in 1762-1763 the two preached, and they obviously preached with considerable power. A concerted attempt was made to establish Methodism among the slaves who had returned from England with Nathaniel Gilbert. These folk succeeded! They are responsible for "the first Methodist chapel in the Torrid Zone."[7]

The Gilbert brothers had great effect in their proclamation of the gospel, telling their hearers of God's love. Eventually Nathaniel gave up his government post and devoted all his time to preaching. The question immediately comes, Why did he not manumit his slaves on the spot? In part, the answer may be that the laws of the island were exceedingly harsh toward freed slaves.[8] Having resigned from the Legislative Assembly, Gilbert became a preacher of note, and Methodism spread throughout Antigua. Slavery, however, was never far from his thoughts; he was obviously searching and reading. Among the antislavery publications he read were those of the Quaker, Anthony Benezet.

Emancipation of slaves being virtually impossible, Gilbert increasingly became an ardent foe of the dread

institution. On October 29, 1768, he wrote Anthony
Benezet:

> I desire to embrace as my brethren all who love the Lord Jesus in
> sincerity. I cannot but think that all true christians [sic] agree in
> fundamenals. Your tracts concerning slavery are very just, and it is a
> matter I have often thought of, even before I became acquainted
> with the truth: your arguments are forcible against purchasing
> slaves, or being any way concerned in that trade.[9]

In all likelihood, it was through Nathaniel Gilbert that
John Wesley was put in touch with Anthony Benezet's
antislavery views. A fortuitous introduction it was!

Gilbert's untimely death, April 20, 1774, left his flock
without a shepherd. Work was continued by Sophia
Campbell and Mary Alley—slaves who *may* have met
Wesley in 1758—and Mary Leadbetter, a teacher. In
1773, Francis Gilbert had written, "Almost the whole
island seems to be stirred up to seek the Lord. Here is
work enough for three preachers."

In 1775 the Methodists of Antigua requested Francis
Asbury to come. On Wednesday, February 22, 1775, he
noted, "I feel inclined to go, and take one of the young
men with me. But there is one obstacle in my way—the
administration of the ordinances."[10]

Eventually, John Baxter did go to Antigua to labor as a
master shipwright at English Harbour. It was not long
before shipbuilding was forgotten as Baxter found all his
time employed in preaching. A new and exciting chapter
had begun in Antigua. On Christmas Day, 1786, Dr.
Thomas Coke arrived at St. Johns, Antigua. It was the
beginning of extensive Methodist witness throughout the
Caribbean.[11] By 1786 the membership of Antigua
comprised 1,569. Only two members were white.

The witness continued—and it was a witness to the
slaves. The year 1793 saw a Methodist membership of
2,420. Of these, only 36 were white.[12]

CHAPTER VI

WESLEY'S COMMENTS ON SLAVERY

*D*uring the mid-years of the eighteenth century John Wesley was engaged in constant, but always well-organized, activity. His Revival was having enormous impact on the people of the British Isles and far beyond. Throughout these years, Wesley's attention frequently turned to the slavery issue and found expression in varied and, at times, amazing manifestations.

The Caribbean appears to have occupied Wesley's thoughts in a number of ways. On November 26, 1758, he noted talking with a lady from Barbados, and a strange conversation it was.

I was well pleased to have some conversation with Mrs. A—t, lately come from Barbadoes. She gave me an account of her poor husband (first a red-hot Predestinarian, talking of God's 'blowing whole worlds to hell,' then a Quaker, now a Deist); as also of the narrow escape which Mr. H. [Wesley Hall] lately had: 'Ten negroes broke into his house; one of whom was upon the point of cutting his throat when E. R. knocked him down with a pewter pot; which put the rest into such confusion that she had time to secure herself and her children, and Mr. H. to leap out of a balcony.'[1]

This bizarre entry by Wesley is an example of his habit of recording all manner of events. The notation does point up his continued interest in people related to the West Indies. It is all the more extraordinary that the next *Journal* entry is the remarkable experience of baptizing the African women from Antigua.

John Newton

John Wesley, the omnivorous reader and writer, always had a pen in his hand (when he was not riding horse or preaching). Among his hundreds of letters, and more especially his letters regarding slavery, it is curious that the name of John Newton does not appear more often.

Newton, the reformed slave ship captain, so gloriously converted, and the author of some of hymnody's greatest, including "Amazing Grace! How Sweet the Sound" and "How Sweet the Name of Jesus Sounds," had become an outspoken foe of slavery. There are several letters from Wesley to Newton, but all of them are regarding theology. Slavery is never mentioned.

Wesley wrote Newton from Liverpool on April 9, 1765: "I have just finished your *Narrative,* a remarkable proof, as you observe, that with God all things are possible. The objection current here, that you talk too much of Mrs. Newton, seems to me of no force at all."[2] The letter continues, all in the vein of doctrine, with emphasis on Scripture.

A long letter, centering on Calvinism, was written May 14, 1765, from Londonderry by Wesley, "Your manner of writing needs no excuse. I hope you will always write in the same manner . . . . You have admirably well expressed what I mean by an opinion contradistinguished from an essential doctrine."[3] Another, from Lewisham, February 28, 1766, concludes with Wesley's mentioning that he has just published *A Plain Account of Christian Perfection*. "If you care to give it a reading, you shall be welcome to a copy. I hope Mrs. Newton and yourself will never forget in your prayers, dear sir, Your affectionate brother and servant."[4]

The April 1, 1766, letter to Newton states: "I do not perceive that there is an hair's breadth difference between us with regard to the nature of Sanctification: only you *express* a little less plainly . . ."[5]

In his August 16, 1769, *Journal* entry, Wesley recorded, "To-day I gave a second reading to that lively book, Mr. Newton's *Account of his own Experience*. There is something very extraordinary therein, but one may account for it without a jot of Predestination. I doubt not but his, as well as Colonel Gardiner's, conversion was an answer to his mother's prayers."[6]

Veritably, the good John Newton *had* been converted! He was later ordained—and that took a bit of doing—and he served at Olney in Buckinghamshire. The famous *Olney Hymns,* published with Cowper in 1779, hold a particular place in the devotional/literary life of the English people. Newton served as rector of a London church. He was a friend of Whitefield, and, alas, it was the Calvinism of both of these distinguished clergymen that Wesley could not abide. Thus it was, the exchange of letters between Wesley and Newton was restricted to theology and the devotional life.

A written dialogue between the two—Newton, author of *Thoughts upon the African Slave Trade,* and Wesley, author of *Thoughts upon Slavery*—on the topic of slavery, would have been exciting. It is a pity such has not appeared. In view of their staunch opposition to slavery and their mutual concern for sanctification, it would be stimulating reading!

Wesley the Student

During the early years of the 1770s, John Wesley was reading extensively in moral philosophy. Slavery was very much a part of the vast problem bedeviling humankind. In point of fact "for many Europeans, as diverse as John Wesley and the Abbé Raynal, the African was an innocent child of nature whose enslavement in America betrayed the very notion of the New World as a land of natural innocence and new hope for mankind."[7] Blacks were portrayed as people of natural virtue and sensitivity "at once oppressed by the worst vices of civilization and yet capable of receiving its greatest benefits."

Wesley was always seeking to find new and fresh information about humanity in general. On Friday, December 17, 1773, he eagerly opened "a celebrated book, a volume of Captain Cook's *Voyages*," with keen anticipation, "I sat down to read it with huge expectation. But how was I disappointed!" The illustrations were inconceivable—too much for an eighteenth-century Oxford M.A., heavily influenced by the Enlightenment. Said an astonished Wesley:

I observed (1) things absolutely incredible: 'A nation without any curiosity'; and, what is stranger still (I fear related with no good design), 'without any sense of shame! Men and women coupling together in the face of the sun, and in the sight of scores of people! Men whose skin, cheeks, and lips are white as milk.' Hume or Voltaire might believe this, but I cannot.

He continued, expressing his sense of social outrage:

I observed (2) things absolutely impossible. To instance in one, for a specimen. A native of Otaheite is said to understand the language of an island eleven hundred degrees distant from it in latitude, besides I know not how many hundreds in longitude! So that I cannot but rank this narrative with that of Robinson Crusoe, and account Tupia to be, in several respects, akin to his man Friday.[8]

Was John Wesley so unsophisticated? No more than a vast number of English people of his time. His cultural views, his moral interpretations, his values, all reflect the *Zeitgeist* wherein he lived.

Mores and life-style of peoples of the Pacific, so graphically portrayed by Captain Cook, were simply beyond Wesley's Puritan understanding. By interesting contrast, he, along with a number of other writers, "compared West Africa to the Garden of Eden, and the inhabitants to man's first parents."[9]

Wesley—Man of Faith

Wesley was not a sociologist in the contemporary use of the term. He was a man of intense faith-orientation. He espoused, and bequeathed to his spiritual descendants, an interpretation of the gospel which was neither restricted by the "immutable decrees" of Calvinsim nor inhibited by the theological hair-splitting of seventeenth- and eighteenth-century Anglicanism. He added a social note to the scheme of salvation. People were saved "to become centers of salvation."[10] Wesley embraced the whole of life and the whole of humankind. "God willeth all men to be saved and to come to the knowledge of the truth." A person filled with the Holy Spirit could not pick and choose areas of devotion or concern, rejecting that which was displeasing. A Christian, as Wesley viewed the Christian life, could not live in Christ and exclude suffering humanity. For Wesley, *sola Scriptura* was infused with "holiness of heart and life."[11] For him "the fulness of faith" demanded a social consciousness. Critics of Wesley's theology, and they were legion, chided him and later Methodists, that his theology was essentially one of good works. It was not! For Wesley, Christ was the only means of salvation;

by Christ alone. Further, the one saved could undergo an assurance of God's indwelling, God's loving presence. From this experience of grace, the believer moved to the outward witness—service—in Christ's name. The life of faith incorporated the warm heart and the world parish.[12] Thus Wesley continued his Revival, ever looking to areas of human need, and Thomas Coke, his close associate in later years, first bishop in American Methodism and "Foreign Minister of Methodism," preached again and again on that choice text, Psalm 68:31: "Ethiopia shall soon stretch out her hands unto God" (KJV).[13]

Meeting with the Societies

Much of Wesley's time was spent with his Societies. This was the heart of the Revival. Here he celebrated the sacraments of baptism and the Lord's Supper, preached, and ministered to the needs of his people.

On Sunday, May 7, 1780, at Whitehaven, Wesley spoke poignantly. "I had an opportunity given me of meeting the select society. I was pleased to find that none of them have lost the pure love of God since they received it first." He went on, discernibly moved, "I was particularly pleased with a poor negro. She semed to be fuller of love than any of the rest. And not only her voice had an unusual sweetness, but her words were chosen and uttered with a peculiar propriety. I never heard, either in England or America, such a negro speaker (man or woman) before."[14] Once more, it is unfortunate her name is not recorded. The event indicates Africans were members of the Societies.

John Wesley was a preacher! He loved to preach! In Sermon LXIX *The Imperfection of Human Knowledge*, he made a vivid plea in graphic language to his day and generation. He was addressing English people of the Enlightenment, asking, "And who cares for thousands, myriads, if not millions, of the wretched Africans? Are not whole droves of these poor sheep (human, if not rational beings!) continually driven to market, and sold, like cattle, into the vilest bondage, without any hope of deliverance but by death?" He repeated his plea, "Who cares for those outcasts of men, the well-known Hottentots?" Wesley then made a special point of the conventional understanding of Hottentot culture:

It is true, a late writer has taken much pains to represent them as a respectable people: But from what motive it is not easy to say; since he himself allows (a specimen of their elegance of manners) that the raw guts of sheep and other cattle are not only some of their choicest food, but also the ornaments of their arms and legs; and (a specimen of their religion) that the son is not counted a man, till he has beat his mother almost to death; and when his father grows old, he fastens him in a little hut, and leaves him there to starve!

The gruesome picture, in Wesley's eyes, caused him to cry out to his own British culture, "O Father of mercies! are not these the works of thy own hands, the purchase of thy Son's blood?"[15]

The sermon reflects Wesley's concern for the Christian message, that it be preached to all peoples, to every nation. It likewise demonstrates Wesley's unrelenting opposition to human enslavement. Too, this message came in Wesley's later life. He was, by this time, leading in the crusade against the slave trade. His prophetic voice was being lifted, and he was being heard.

This particular sermon was prepared in Bristol, dated March 5, 1784, and published in the *Arminian Magazine,* June and July 1784. There is no record of his ever having preached it. Although it is in sermonic form, with major divisions and subdivisions, it is in effect a sermonic essay, with slavery brought in as a subsidiary element.

Friday, March 10, 1786, found Wesley in the Bristol area. He recorded, "I baptized a young negro, who appeared to be deeply serious and much affected; as indeed did the whole congregation."[16] Blacks were part of the fellowship, perhaps not in large numbers, yet they were present.

Perhaps one of the most exciting preaching experiences Wesley recorded took place in Bristol, that center for so much of the coming and going of slave ships. He would have realized that in the early days of the slave trade, Bristol was a chief port for these vessels. He had "two or three quiet days" and concluded by finishing "my sermon upon Conscience." On "*Tuesday* [March 4, 1788] I gave notice of my design to preach on Thursday evening upon (what is now the general topic) Slavery." Lo, when Thursday arrived the house was filled "from end to end" and all sorts and conditions of people were on hand, "high and low, rich and poor." It was, without doubt, an eclectic gathering. It was manifestly an excited congregation. Wesley was an acknowledged leader among the opponents of slavery—everyone knew it. No one was disappointed with the sermon. The text was Genesis 9:27.

I preached on that ancient prophecy. 'God shall enlarge Japheth. And he shall dwell in the tents of Shem; and Canaan shall be his servant.'

All was well, thus far:

About the middle of the discourse, while there was on every side attention still as night, a vehement noise arose, none could tell why, and shot like lightning through the whole congregation. The terror and confusion were inexpressible. You might have imagined it was a city taken by storm. The people rushed upon each other with the utmost violence; the benches were broken in pieces, and nine-tenths of the congregation appeared to be struck with the same panic.

Suddenly, all was quiet: "In about six minutes the storm ceased, almost as suddenly as it rose, and, all being calm, I went on without the least interruption."

Wesley concluded:

It was the strangest incident of the kind I ever remember; and I believe none can account for it without supposing some preternatural influence. Satan fought, lest his kingdom should be delivered up.

He went on:

We set *Friday* apart as a day of fasting and prayer that God would remember those poor outcasts of men; and (what seems impossible with men, considering the wealth and power of their oppressors) make a way for them to escape, and break their chains in sunder.[17]

This dramatic and little recognized service may represent what was taking place in Great Britain. The slavery issue was highly emotional—just as it was in America in the fifties and sixties—and John Wesley was playing an important role.

CHAPTER
VII

BENEZET: A QUAKER
OPPONENT OF SLAVERY

*T*he year 1772 was a time of discovery. Slavery was obviously on Wesley's mind that important year. It was probably on the mind of every thinking or concerned person in England. Lord Chief Justice Mansfield (Charles Wesley's old schoolfellow) rendered his famous decision regarding a slave, an American Negro, James Somerset.[1] It was "England's most famous slave case." For centuries native serfdom had been part of English law, dating from the Magna Carta. Negroes could be held as slaves on English soil. No more! An ancient law was now altered.

On June 22, 1772, in the Somerset Case, Lord Mansfield's declaration in the Court of King's Bench, *fiat justitia, ruat caelum* (let justice be done, though the heavens fall), was "that whenever and wherever a slave set foot on English soil he was from that moment free." This decision was treated by some as *obiter dictum* (an unofficial expression of opinion). It was far more than that. What was the meaning of "English territory"? For example, Did it include the deck of an English ship?[2]

A number of brilliant legal experts took part in the Somerset case. One was the noted Granville Sharp, "son of Thomas Sharp, prebendary of Durham, and grandson of John Sharp, Archbishop of York," a distinguished individual from a distinguished family. In 1769 he published *Representation of the Injustice . . . of tolerating Slavery.* This influential publication originated in Sharp's defense of Jonathan Strong, an escaped slave, in 1765. Another important lawyer involved was Francis Hargrave. In 1772 he published *An Argument in the Case of James Sommersett, a Negro.*[3] John Wesley carefully read both works, and later made use of them, with appreciation for Sharp and Hargrave.

In spite of Lord Mansfield's ruling, the selling of slaves continued in Bristol until the close of 1792. Indeed, "the conditions of English social economy and agricultural laborers rendered negro slavery almost superfluous; and that in the British West Indies, where climate and other conditions resembled those of the southern United States, negro slavery continued till 1834."[4]

Wesley's Reading List

It was Monday, February 10, 1772, that John Wesley made his way to Dorking. Obviously the good man took a number of hours to engage in a wide variety of reading matter. "I read Mr. Jones's ingenious tract upon Clean and Unclean Beasts." This would have been William Jones' *Zoologica Ethica: A Disquisition concerning the Mosaic Distinction of Animals into Clean and Unclean,* published in London, 1771. "He really seems to prove his point," said Wesley, " . . . that there is a . . . deeper design in that part of the Levitical Law than is commonly understood."[5]

The following day the remarkable Mr. Wesley changed his reading subjects. He looked into Laurence Sterne's work and described it in colorful language:

I casually took a volume of what is called *A Sentimental Journey Through France and Italy. Sentimental!* what is that? It is not English; he might as well say *Continental.* It is not sense. It conveys no determinate idea; yet one fool makes many . . . . However, the book agrees full well with the title, for one is as queer as the other. For oddity, uncouthness, and unlikeness to all the world beside, I suppose, the writer is without a rival.[6]

So much for Laurence Sterne!

On Wednesday, February 12, as he was coming back from Dorking, Wesley made quite a contrasting entry in his *Journal:*

In returning I read a very different book, published by an honest Quaker, on that execrable sum of all villanies, commonly called the Slave-trade. I read of nothing like it in the heathen world, whether ancient or modern; and it infinitely exceeds, in every instance of barbarity, whatever Christian slaves suffer in Mahometan countries.[7]

It was a discovery! It was a revelation! Who was this "honest Quaker" whose book had such an impact on John Wesley?

Anthony Benezet

Anthony Benezet was born January 31, 1713, in San Quenten, Picardy, France, son of Jean Etienne Benezet. The family is described:

His parents were among the most noted and wealthy persons of that time. They associated themselves with those protestants [sic] who had been contemptuously denominated Huguenots on the revocation of the edict of Nantz, and who became obnoxious to the unparalled fury of Romish bigotry during the reign of Lewis XIV.[8]

This persecution caused the family to flee to Rotterdam in 1715; here they remained only a short time. They then made their way to London where they established a home for sixteen years and where Anthony was educated, became an apprentice in a mercantile house, and, of greater importance, came under Quaker influence. At age fourteen he joined the Society of Friends.

The Benezet family sailed for Philadelphia in 1731. Eighteen-year-old Anthony was "well recommended by divers Friends." For a time he was with his brothers John, Philip, and Daniel in the import business. The *Pennsylvania Gazette* frequently carried advertisements for Philip Benezet's business. The family was doing well.

In May of 1736 Anthony Benezet married Joyce Marriott[9] of Burlington, New Jersey. The union lasted forty-eight years. Anthony was taking a long and careful look at his life, his future. It was undeniable that the merchant's life was not for him. He had been employed at Wilmington, Delaware, for a period, but his real dream was to become a teacher, and to that end he went to the Germantown Academy. In 1742 he began teaching in the Friends' English Public School in Philadelphia (later designated the William Penn Charter School), and remained there for twelve years. In 1755 he founded a girls' school. He was now in his element: a school, a teacher!

During these years Benezet became deeply concerned—in good Quaker fashion—about reports from Africa and the Caribbean regarding the slave trade. He soon joined with fellow Quaker, John Woolman, in writing against the reprehensible business. He continued the work after Woolman's death, publishing articles and pamphlets. Most of these were distributed without charge. He began a wide correspondence with Granville Sharp, William Wilberforce, and Thomas Clarkson in England. Benezet's knowledge of French permitted exchange of letters with the Abbé Raynal in France. The greats of the earth did not deter him. The

Countess of Huntingdon was one, to say nothing of the queens of England, France, and Portugal. Add to this list Frederick the Great and a memorial to the King of Great Britain. In America there were Patrick Henry and Henry Laurens, "President of the Congress of the United States." Among his close associates were Benjamin Franklin, Dr. Benjamin Rush, Dr. Caspar Wistar, and the Comte de Lucerne—ambassador from Louis XVI to the United States.[10] Among his less affluent associates, Benezet had some Methodist friends, the noted preacher and his wife, Captain and Mrs. Thomas Webb.

When the French in Arcadia were expelled in 1756, some five hundred made their way to Philadelphia. Always concerned about oppressed people, Benezet and the Quaker community welcomed them.

In addition to his teaching, Benezet turned with increased zeal to writing. From Germantown, in 1759, he published *Observations on the Enslaving, Importing, and Purchasing of Negroes.*[11] This work appeared in two editions. In 1762, from Philadelphia, came *A Short Account of that Part of Africa, inhabited by the Negroes.* It was translated into German in 1763. It was obviously an important publication, going through five editions. It is possible that this was the book Wesley read on February 12, 1772.

It was the 1766 publication, from Philadelphia, of *A Caution and Warning to Great Britain and her Colonies, in a short Representation of the calamitous State of the enslaved Negroes in British Dominions* "which created not a little stir on this continent and in Europe."[12] It enjoyed a remarkable response, six editions. It was a 144-page volume, stressing "the evils of slavery and the inconsistency of the practice with the religion of Christ."[13]

It might also be shown, that it destroys the bonds of natural affection and interest, whereby mankind in general are united; that it introduces idleness, discourages marriage, corrupts the youth, ruins and debauches morals, excites continual apprehensions of dangers, and frequent alarms.[14]

This, too, may have been the work read by Wesley. It certainly was a significant study. The 1766 Yearly Meeting of Friends in Philadelphia approved the treatise and sent at least two thousand copies to the Society of Friends in London, requesting that it be reprinted in England (it would have been easy for Wesley to have obtained a copy).

That same year, 1766, Benezet moved to Burlington, New Jersey, his wife's home, where he hoped to remain in retirement. Not so; poor Benezet would be deprived of such leisure. He returned to Philadelphia and resumed an even heavier schedule. The year 1771 was especially important. It saw the publication of *Historical Account of Guinea*. This, also, may have been the book Wesley read on that significant return from Dorking. Wesley did write Benezet after reading the particular work (whether it was *A Short Account . . . of Africa* or *A Caution* or *Historical Account of Guinea*). It is possible that Wesley did not see *Historical Account of Guinea* until later, when Benezet sent him a copy of the Philadelphia edition, or Sharp a London edition, who noted, "I sent Copies to all the Judges, . . .& many others."[15]

Historical Account of Guinea proved to be a major publication. This book of 197 pages went through many editions and was widely circulated.

After hearing from Wesley regarding *Historical Account of Guinea*, Benezet wrote to Granville Sharp on May 14, 1772. An amazing communication it was, the first letter to Sharp, informing him that a portion of his book had already been incorporated in *Historical Account of Guinea*.

I have long been desirous to advise with such well-disposed persons in England, as have a prospect of the iniquity of the slave trade, and are concerned to prevent its continuance. And I should have wrote thee thereon, had I known how to direct; particularly as I have taken the freedom to republish a part of thy acceptable, and I trust serviceable, treatise. But now, . . . I make free affectionately to salute thee, and to send thee some copies of a treatise lately published here on that iniquitous traffick, giving the best account of its origin, progress, &c., we have been able to procure.[16]

He added, "My friend John Westly [*sic*] promises he will consult with thee about the expediency of some weekly publication, in the newspapers, on the origin, nature, and dreadful effects of the slave trade."[17]

Granville Sharp made a gracious reply to Benezet. He would have had good reason to be angry at outright plagiarism as well as his right to demand why a request had not first been made—Benezet's excuse about not knowing "how to direct" was weak. From Old Jewry, London, August 21, 1772, he wrote Benezet, "You need not have made an apology for having abridged my book." He went on, "I send you a copy of your own book as reprinted here, and some other pamphlets lately published on the subject. . . ."[18] (Unauthorized "borrowing" of published material was a common eighteenth-century practice.)

There was more. Wesley wrote Sharp, stating that he desired to "write against the slave trade," just as he had promised Benezet. Sharp responded by sending Wesley "a large bundle of books and papers on the subject."[19] This may be the beginning of John Wesley's systematic investigation of the trade. He had abhorred the practice since his Georgia days, but now his research got under way.

More publications were to come from Benezet's pen. In 1774, there was *The Mighty Destroyer Displaced*, an essay on immoderate use of liquor. In 1778 he wrote *Serious Considerations on Several Important Subjects, viz: On*

War and Its Inconsistence with the Gospel. Observations on Slavery. And Remarks on the Nature and bad Effects of Spirituous Liquors, reproducing and editing portions of *Thoughts upon Slavery* (one note may be from John Newton). *The Plain Path to Christian Perfection* came in 1780. He also wrote a *Short Account of the People Called Quakers: Their Rise, Religious Principles and Settlement in America.* In 1784 he published, anonymously, *Some Observations on the Situation, Disposition, and Character of the Indian Natives of This Continent.* Patently, his concern for humanity was broad. It is sad that he and Wesley never met face to face. The exchange of views would have made good copy for the eighteenth-century press.

Benezet "was small; his countenance was composed of strong and interesting features, and though his face beamed with benignant animation, it was far from being handsome."[20] A friend once suggested his portrait be painted. *"O! no, no, my ugly face shall not go down to posterity."* For Benezet, superfluity in dress was unthinkable; "his clothing being made in the most simple manner, and of some material [cotton velvet] selected on account of the durability of its texture." He lived in one of the first brick dwellings erected in Philadelphia, on the north side of Chestnut, between Third and Fourth Streets. "But humble as they were, his dwelling was the resort, and his hospitable table has been spread for entertainment of some of the worthiest characters of the country, whilst few foreigners of distinction who came to Philadelphaia, left it without visiting him."[21]

The concluding years of Benezet's life found him teaching in a school for Blacks. At his death, Benezet willed his property to his wife for her lifetime. At her death the estate would be used to endow the school, with the Overseers of the Friends' Public School as the trustees. The institution was later renamed "Benezet House" of Locust Street, Philadelphia.

Benezet died May 3, 1784. He had earlier expressed his disapproval "of the often over-rated testimonies which were recorded of the dead." Should his desires in this matter be disregarded, *"they may say,"*

ANTHONY BENEZET

was

A Poor Creature,

and

THROUGH DIVINE FAVOUR,

was

Enabled to Know It.[22]

The name of Benezet appears in Wesley's October 31, 1784, letter to Francis Asbury. Wesley mentions an obstreperous preacher, John Helton (misread in the text of the letter as John Hilton), who in 1778 wrote "Reasons for Quitting the Methodist Society," a reply to Wesley's "Letter to a Person Joined with the Quakers." Wesley noted to Asbury that Helton's "harmless performance" would soon die and be forgotten, adding, "I don't believe Anthony Benezet ever recommended it."[23] Wesley is acknowledging Benezet's importance as a Quaker, rather than his general worth in the field of slavery reform. Nonetheless, Wesley clearly held Benezet's opinion in high esteem.

Benezet's Study of Guinea

The work carried a somewhat turgid title, typical of the eighteenth century, and certainly true-to-type for Benezet:

Some Historical Account of GUINEA, Its Situation, Produce and the general Disposition of its Inhabitants. With An inquiry into the Rise and Progress of the Slave-Trade, its Nature and lamentable Effects. Also A Re-publication of the Sentiments of several Authors of Note, on this interesting Subject; particularly an Extract of a Treatise, by Granville Sharp. By Anthony Benezet. Philadelphia: Printed by Joseph Crukshank, in Third-street, opposite the Work-house. M,DCC,LXXI

The first 144 pages cover the work by Benezet; the remaining portion—pages 1-53—is by Sharp and others. Unhappily, the outline, or lack of it, leaves much to be desired. In a sense, Benezet is more of a compiler than an author. There is much duplication and overlapping of data.[24] Benezet's earlier publications, *A Short Account of that Part of Africa, inhabited by Negroes* of 1762 and *A Caution and Warning to Great Britain and her Colonies* of 1766, are reflected in this volume.

The material, garnered by Benezet, is largely an aggregation of the notes, journals, and commentaries of people who had traveled in Africa and the Caribbean, as well as those familiar with slave conditions in the British colonies in North America—a wide and varied assortment. These are noted, usually by name but without identification. Special writings are sometimes cited. Among the references (as Benezet spells the names): James Barbot, an agent general to the French African Company; Andrew Brue, also of the French Company; Francis Moor, who in 1735 was sent out from England with the African Company. William Smith went out in 1726 for the African Company, to survey their settlements on the coast of Guinea. There are notes by M. Adamson, who made a voyage to Senegal as correspondent for the Royal Academy of Science in Paris, 1749–1753, recording natural and philosophical observations on the Senegal and Gambia rivers. Peter Kolben's account of the Cape of Good

Hope is used. Others cited are: Thomas Philips, Griffith Hughes, Thomas Jefferey, Sir Hans Sloan, Father Tachard a French Jesuit, William Bosman. Benezet's introduction clearly states his thesis:

The slavery of the Negroes having, of late, drawn the attention of many serious minded people; several tracts have been published setting forth its inconsistancy with every christian [sic] and moral virtue, which its [sic] hoped will have weight with the judicious; especially at a time when the liberties of mankind are become so much the subject of general attention . . . that the iniquity of this practice may become effectually apparent, to those in whose power it may be, to put a stop to any farther progress therein. . . . And here it will not be improper to premise, that . . . there is any real foundation for that argument, so commonly advanced, in vindication of that trade viz. *"That the slavery of the Negroes took its rise from a desire, in the purchasers, to save the lives of such of them as were taken captives in war, who would otherwise have been sacrificed to the implacable revenge of their conquerors."*[25]

In the first chapter, the emphasis is on Guinea as a vital area of West Africa, rich in beauty and natural resources.

That part of Africa from which the Negroes are sold to be carried into slavery, commonly known by the name of Guinea, extends along the coast three or four thousand miles. Beginning at the river Senegal, situated about the 17th degree of north latitude, being the nearest part of Guinea, as well to Europe, as to North America; from thence to the river Gambia, and in a southerly course to cape Sierra Leona, comprehends a coast of about seven hundred Miles; being the same tract for which Queen Elizabeth granted charters to the first traders to that coast: From Sierra Leona, the land of Guinea takes a turn to the eastward, extending that course about fifteen hundred miles, including those several divisions known by the name of *the Grain Coast; the Ivory Coast; the Gold Coast and the Slave Coast, with the large kingdom of Benin.* From thence the land runs southward along the coast about twelve hundred miles, which contains the *kingdoms of Congo and Angola;* there the trade for slaves ends. From which to the southermost cape of Africa, called the cape of Good Hope, the country is settled by Caffers and Hottentots: Who have never been concerned in the making or selling of slaves.[26]

Benezet has given here the several territories for which Africa was known by the Europeans and Americans. Grain, ivory, gold, and slaves could be gotten on the appropriately designated coast.

One of Benezet's chief points is that this wide territory is far from being barren. Said Andrew Brue, "the farther you go from the Sea, the country on the river seems the more fruitful and well improved; abounding with Indian corn, pulse, fruit, &c. Here are vast meadows, which feed large herds of great and small cattle, and poultry numerous." Of the population, there are the Fulis, and especially the Mandingos "the most numerous nation on the *Gambia*."[27]

Guinea "affords an easy Living to its Inhabitants, with but little Toil. The Climate agrees well with the Natives; but extreamly unhealthful to the Europeans." The people enjoy good health; there is a variety of fresh food; few clothes are required. They "might have lived happy, if not disturbed by the Europeans; more especially, if these last had used such endeavours as their christian [*sic*] profession requires, to communicate to the ignorant Africans that superior knowledge which providence has favoured them with."[28]

Benezet progresses down the coast, describing the several sections. He then moves to a discussion of the coming of the Arabs, then the Portuguese, and then the English. He cites Montesquieu, Morgan Godwyn, and Bartolomé de Las Casas, all who made an attempt to thwart the practice of slavery. In Las Casas' case, he befriended the American Indians, at the expense of the Africans, a position he later regretted.

A considerable amount of attention is given to the brutality of the system, and the numbers of Africans taken. The sum and substance is the intense human tragedy. Far from being removed from a culture barren, these Africans have culture and religion. Indeed, very beautiful African concepts, but, of course, not Christian ideas and ideals.

The subsequent chapters deal with various aspects of the sections of Guinea, such as the soil and the products, or the tribal divisions, as the reference from William Smith:

That the Gold Coast and Slave Coasts are divided into different districts, some of which are governed by their chiefs or kings; the others being more of the nature of a commonwealth, are governed by some of the principal men, called Caboceros, . . . are properly denominated civil fathers; whose province is to take care of the wellfare [*sic*] of the city or village and to appease tumults.[29]

Unfortunately, this order of government has been broken since the coming of the Europeans.

Benezet concludes with a plea, "What shall be done with those Negroes already imported and born in our families? Must they be sent to Africa?" This poses problems aplenty. He goes on to say, "That all farther importation of slaves be absolutely prohibited; and as those born among us, after serving so long as may appear to be equitable, let them by law be declared free."[30]

Benezet feels it is essential to respond to a widespread myth: the warm climate of the West Indies will not permit white people to labor there. Richard Ligon, who resided in Barbados during 1647–1650 insists there were "fifty thousand souls on that island, besides Negroes."[31]

Benezet makes his case. It is not his eyewitness account, but he cites sufficient witnesses to make his story come alive. It is an important contribution. John Wesley certainly found it so.

The second portion of the volume:

Extracts from a Representation of the Injustice and Dangerous Tendency of Tolerating SLAVERY, or Admitting the least Claim of private Property in the Persons of Men in England by Granville Sharp. London: Printed MDCCLXIX Philadelphia: Re-printed by Joseph Crukshank, in Third-street, opposite the Work-house. M DCC LXXI.

The essay by Sharp is dynamic. He had been associated with the Mansfield decision, defending Somerset and becoming a leading foe of slavery in Great Britain.

There followed:

Extracts from the writings of several noted Authors, on the Subject of the Slavery of the Negroes, viz. George Wallace, Francis Hutcheson, James Foster.

Next was:

Extracts From an Address in the Virginia Gazette, of March 19, 1767.

The closing treatise:

Extract of a Sermon, Preached by the Bishop of Gloucester, Before the Society for the Propagation of the Gospel, at their anniversary meeting, on the 21st of February, 1766.

The work concludes with the index. (See chapter 1 of this book for additional portions of Benezet's *Historical Account of Guinea.*)

CHAPTER
VIII

WESLEY'S THOUGHTS
UPON SLAVERY, 1774

*J*ohn Wesley had a social conscience. In his *Preface* to *List of Poetical Works* he insisted:

The gospel of Christ knows of no religion, but social; no holiness but social holiness. "Faith working by love" is the length and breadth and depth and height of Christian perfection. "This commandment have we from Christ, that he who loves God, love his brother also;" and that we manifest our love "by doing good unto all men; especially to them that are of the household of faith."[1]

In his Sermon 24 *Upon our Lord's Sermon on the Mount, Discourse the Fourth,* John Wesley maintained: "Christianity is essentially a social religion, and that to turn it into a solitary one is to destroy it; . . . that to conceal this religion is impossible, as well as utterly contrary to the design of its author."[2]

Thoughts upon Slavery is John Wesley answering a major social ill. Using the best methods of eighteenth-century scholarship, plus logic and common sense, he makes his case and adds to it the gospel of Jesus Christ.

Wesley knew what he was doing. The year was 1744, and using Benezet as his guide, Wesley had carefully prepared his major attack. Slavery was morally indefensible—to say nothing of its being completely at variance with the Christian gospel. Wesley thus published his *Thoughts upon Slavery,* and the war was on! To say that *Thoughts upon Slavery* is an abridgment of Benezet's work is a serious mistake. True, Wesley editorialized, and took sections, but a comparison of the two works gives clear evidence that there is more of Wesley in *Thoughts upon Slavery* than he has been given credit. *Thoughts upon Slavery* is Wesley, carefully sorting out his facts—and he has many sources—then presenting the evidence to make his argument. It is a masterful piece. Its success was as enormous as it was important. Its influence was widespread.

Benezet's *Historical Account of Guinea* was an inspiration for Wesley, and Wesley employed it for about 30 percent of *Thoughts upon Slavery. Historical Account of Guinea* lacked good organization. It could have benefited by Wesley's systematic approach to the subject. *Thoughts upon Slavery* was carefully structured.

Design of the Text

Wesley's format is in five Sections, each with numbered subsections, all prepared in his usual systemic style, a gestalt easy to follow.

Section I is essentially an introduction, with a precise definition of slavery presented in subsections 1 and 2. Subsections 3 and 4 provide a brief history of the institution of slavery. Most of this material comes from Granville Sharp. Francis Hargrave's *An Argument in the Case of James Sommersett, a Negro,* is likewise paraphrased. There is a juristic note throughout this Section, reflecting the original documents.

Section II begins with an introduction by Wesley:

Such is the nature of slavery; such the beginning of Negro slavery in America. But some may desire to know what kind of country it is from which the Negroes are brought; what sort of men, of what temper and behaviour are they in their own country; and in what manner they are generally procured, carried to, and treated in, America.

Subsection 1 continues the same questioning, What kind of country "is that from whence they are brought? Is it so remarkably horrid, dreary, and barren, that it is a kindness to deliver them out of it?" The purpose is to describe Africa, the *real* Africa, from which slaves are procured, along with descriptions of the general life of the people. Almost all of subsectons 2 through 11 constitute paraphrases from Benezet's *Historical Account of Guinea*.

Beginning with the second half of subsection 11, Wesley presents a powerful summation.

Upon the whole, therefore, the Negroes who inhabit the coast of Africa, from the river Senegal to the southern bounds of Angola, are so far from being the stupid, senseless, brutish, lazy barbarians, the fierce, cruel, perfidious savages they have been described, that, on the contrary, they are represented, by them who have no motive to flatter them, as remarkably sensible, considering the few advantages they have for improving their understanding; as industrious to the highest degree, perhaps more so than any other natives of so warm a climate; as fair, just, and honest in all their dealings, unless where white men have taught them to be otherwise; and as far more mild, friendly, and kind to strangers, than any of our forefathers were. *Our forefathers!* Where shall we find at this day, among the fair-faced natives of Euope, a nation generally practicing the justice, mercy, and truth, which are found among these poor Africans? Suppose the preceding accounts are true (which I see no reason or pretence to doubt of,) and we may leave England and France, to seek genuine honesty in Benin, Congo, or Angola.

Section III is chiefly Wesley's. His intention is to portray "In what manner they are generally procured, carried to, and treated in, America." Wesley makes use of Benezet's two works, *Historical Account of Guinea* and a page from *A Short Account . . . of Africa.* He likewise employs Sharp's *Representation* "and this from the original rather than from the excerpt given in Benezet's *Guinea.*"[3]

Throughout this Section Wesley made pointed observations. His particular concern is the brutality of the Europeans. He "made effective use of images of the most sadistic torture."[4] His conclusions: subsection 2 "That their own parents sell them is utterly false: Whites, not Blacks, are without natural affection!" Subsection 4 maintains, with razor-sharp irony, "Such is the manner wherein the Negroes are procured! Thus the Christians preach the Gospel to the Heathens!" Subsection 6 is summed up, "So that it is no wonder, so many should die in the passage; but rather, that any survive it." In subsection 7 Wesley asks, in lines worthy of Shakespeare, "Did the Creator intend that the noblest creatures in the visible world should live such a life as this?" Wesley then quotes Milton's *Paradise Lost*, v. 153, "Are these thy glorious work, Parent of Good?"

The concluding half of *Thoughts upon Slavery* is chiefly from Wesley. It is a brilliant summation of the practice of slavery.

Section IV, subsection 1, begins, "This is the plain, unaggravated matter of fact. Such is the manner wherein our African slaves are procured; such the manner wherein they are removed from their native land, and wherein they are treated in our plantations." He continues, "I would now inquire, whether these things can be defended, on the principles of even heathen honesty [a favorite phrase of Wesley]; whether they can be reconciled (setting the Bible out of the question) with any degree of either justice or mercy." His point is that no authorization can be made by law to substantiate slavery. Subsection 2, "The grand plea is 'They are authorized by law.' " Wesley is quick to point out, "Notwithstanding ten thousand laws, right is right, and wrong is wrong still." He then makes pointed reference to the vicious treatment, concluding, in subsection 3, "I strike at the root of this complicated villany; I absolutely deny all slave-holding to be consistent with any degree of natural justice." Next he turns to the celebrated "Judge Blackstone"—William Blackstone's famous *Commentaries on the Laws of England* —pointing out the three ancient origins of slavery: capture in war, self-sale, and birth. Wesley proceeds to abridge, heavily, Blackstone, Volume I:411-13. Wesley may have taken the material from Sharp's *Representation*, pp. 141-44 (but Wesley did know Blackstone firsthand.)[5]

Wesley then stresses the sum and substance of the actual motive in the slave trade, the cause célèbre for the vendors in human flesh: "to get money." He clearly articulates, in subsection 4, "the whole and sole spring of their motions."

Wesley is at his eloquent best as he graphically illustrates, in subsection 5, business ethics of eighteenth-century England.

Fifty years ago, one meeting an eminent Statesman in the lobby of the House of Commons, said, "You have been long talking about justice and equity. Pray which is this bill; equity or justice?" He answered very short and plain, "D--n justice; it is necessity."

Wesley then makes his point:

Here also the slave-holder fixes his foot; here he rests the strength of his cause. "If it is not quite right, yet it must be so; there is an absolute necessity for it. It is necessary we should procure slaves; and when we have procured them, it is necessary to use them with severity, considering their stupidity, stubbornness and wickedness."

Was it really necessary, in securing wealth, "to violate all the laws of justice, mercy, and truth"? asked Wesley. In subsection 6, Wesley replies to the old argument that "slaves are necessary for the cultivation of our islands; inasmuch as white men are not able to labour in hot climates." Wesley fell back on his Georgia experiences, insisting, "I and my family (eight in number) did employ all our spare time there, in felling of trees and clearing of ground, as hard labour as any Negro need be employed in. The German family [Moravians], likewise, forty in number, were employed in all manner of labour. And this was so far from impairing our health, that we all continued perfectly well, while the idle ones round about us were swept away as with a pestilence." Whites, quite as much as Blacks, were able to withstand the hot climate and hard, manual work. In subsection 7 Wesley declared:

Better no trade, than trade procured by villany. It is far better to have no wealth, than to gain wealth at the expense of virtue. Better is honest poverty, than all the riches bought by the tears, and sweat, and blood of our fellow creatures.

Wesley cites, in subsection 9, the individual he learned of in America, Hugh Bryan[6] of South Carolina, who utilized "mildness and gentleness" and consequently his Negroes "loved and reverenced him as a father, and cheerfully obeyed him out of love." (Wesley here reflects his eighteenth-century naïveté.) He was responding to those who insisted ferocity was necessary because of the Negro's supposed "stupidity, stubborness and wickedness."

Section V is Wesley's writing, and pointed writing it is. He seeks "to make a little application of the proceeding observations." He applies common sense, wit, and logic. He implores the captains of slave ships, in subsection 3, "Whatever you lose, lose not your soul: Nothing can countervail that loss. Immediately quit the horrid trade: At all events, be an honest man."

Wesley then pleads with the merchants, in subsection 4, "Have no more any part in this detestable business. Instantly leave it to those unfeeling wretches who 'Laugh at human nature and compassion!'[7] Be you a man, not a wolf, a devourer of the human species!"

In the following subsection, 5, Wesley turns to the upper classes, "And this equally concerns every gentleman that has an estate in our American plantations; yea, all slave-holders, of whatever rank and degree." He calls them "men-buyers" who are "exactly on a level with men-stealers." He paused, and continued, "You therefore are guilty, yea, principally guilty, of all these frauds, robberies, and murders. You are the spring that puts the rest in motion."

In subsection 6, Wesley is at his vibrant best, "Liberty is the right of every human creature, as soon as he breathes the vital air; and no human law can deprive him of that right which he derives from the law of nature." He drives his point home, "Away with all whips, all chains, all compulsion!"

In subsection 7 Wesley brings his dramatic conclusion. It is a plea to the loving, just, reconciling Deity: "Are not these also the work of thine own hands, the purchase of thy Son's blood? . . . Thou Saviour of all, make them free, that they may be free indeed!" He then quotes from his brother Charles Wesley's poem of 1758, "For the Heathen," third stanza.

Thoughts upon Slavery gives rise to a fundamental question, Does Wesley, as does Benezet, romanticize Africa? Are there too many shades of Rousseau's *Émile*, "God makes all things good; man meddles with them and they become evil"? Is there the Noble Savage? What of *Paul and Virginia*? Has the Age of Reason created stylized figures, replacing authentic human beings? In short, does Wesley discount the basic problems inherent in all cultures and civilizations? After all, more than one African chief sold captive enemies into slavery. Has Wesley idealized Africa into the Garden of Eden—the Garden prior to the Fall?

Again, the answer lies in eighteenth-century rationalism which blamed Western culture for the stain of sin. Also, Wesley, like an expert barrister, establishes his case against the degradation inflicted upon millions of innocent Africans. If Wesley had a propensity to overwrite, it resulted from his sense of moral outrage at the inhuman slave trade.

Publication

John Wesley sent a preliminary draft of *Thoughts upon Slavery* to Granville Sharp, requesting his comments. Sharp replied on December 20, 1773:

Dear sir, I have perused with great satisfaction your little tract against slavery, and am far from thinking that any alteration is necessary. You have very judiciously brought together and digested . . . some of the principal facts cited by my friend Mr. Benezet and others, which you corroborate with some circumstances within your own knowledge; and have very sensibly drawn up the sum of the whole argument into a small compass, which infinitely increases the power and effect of it . . .[8]

Sharp offered good business counsel, advising Wesley it would be wise not to imprint *Thoughts upon Slavery* as part of a collection of similar essays being published by Dilly. Wesley's work would enrich the others, nonetheless *Thoughts upon Slavery* "will certainly have much more weight with many persons if it be separately printed, and published with your name."

On January 7, 1774, Granville Sharp wrote to Anthony Benezet regarding *Thoughts upon Slavery*:

A few days ago he [John Wesley] sent me his manuscript to peruse; which is *well drawn up*, and he has reduced the substance of the argument respecting the gross iniquity of that trade into a very small compass; *his evidence*, however, seems chiefly extracted from the authors quoted in your several publications.[9]

Thoughts upon Slavery came from Robert Hawes' press in Lamb Street, London, in January or February of 1774. It was a pamphlet of fifty-three pages in octavo (pages about six-by-nine inches). It sold for a shilling. Sharp had suggested to Wesley that it come out in a smaller—pocket—edition, duodecimo (pages five-by-seven-and-one-half inches). Part of the pamphlet's success was that it had immediate distribution by Methodist preachers throughout Britain.

Thoughts upon Slavery speedily made its way to America. Wesley himself sent a copy to Benezet, probably in February or March. On May 23 the "honest Quaker" replied (the letter was carried by William Dillwyn, a pupil of Benezet):

The Tract thou has lately published entitled, Thoughts on Slavery, afforded me much satisfaction. I was the more especially glad to see it, as the circumstances of the times made it necessary that something on that most weighty subject, not large, but striking and pathetic, should now be published. Wherefore I immediately agreed with the Printer to have it republished here.[10]

Thus the first American edition was published the same year that it came from the press in England— 1774. It was printed by Benezet's regular agent, Joseph Crukshank. It is remarkable that in so short a time Benezet was to make such wide use of *Thoughts upon Slavery* as part of his compilation *The Potent Enemies of America Laid Open*. The American edition appeared: John Wesley, A.M., *Thoughts Upon Slavery* (London,

Printed: Re-printed in Philadelphia, with notes, and sold by Joseph Crukshank. MD,CC,LXXIV.) It was a small volume of eighty-three pages—six-and-one-fourth inches by three-and-one-fourth inches. It is indeed a fascinating volume. *Thoughts upon Slavery* is reprinted in the first fifty-seven pages. A number of these are filled with copious notes by Benezet. There is also a discussion on slavery taken from Edward Bancroft, an "*English* physician, who resided some years in that part of *America*, called *Dutch Guiana*." It concludes on page 79. Pages 80-83 form an "Extract of a Sermon preached by the Bishop of Gloucester, before the Society for the Propagation of the Gospel at their anniversary meeting, on the 21st of February, 1766." It is the same document printed in Benezet's *Historical Account of Guinea.*

It is interesting that Benezet rushed to get *Thoughts upon Slavery* into print in America. It appears he had few qualms about adding his own notes and other material. Of course, he might have said the same about Wesley's use of his material.

Copies of *Thoughts upon Slavery* were soon distributed on the Continent. The treatise became widespread. People were, ere long, writing, as well as talking, about *Thoughts upon Slavery*. Sharp wrote to Dr. Benjamin Rush that he was sending two copies "of Mr. Westley's [*sic*] Tract ag't. Slavery"[11] to Philadelphia. John Horton wrote Charles Wesley, on February 28, 1774: "The Tract on Slavery I saw as soon as published, and expected to have seen your supplement to it; about three hundred were given away at your brother's expense."[12]

Three more editions of *Thoughts upon Slavery* appeared in England, this time in the smaller duodecimo, of twenty-eight pages, which sold for twopence each. On May 6, 1774, Wesley wrote, from Whitehaven to London: "I could have sold, if I had had them before the day, more than five hundred *Thoughts on Slavery.* You should directly send all that remain but ten or twenty, to meet me at Edinburgh, Newcastle, and Scarborough."[13]

In 1775 *Thoughts upon Slavery* was reprinted in Dublin. The original shilling octavo edition continued on sale for a number of years, along with other editions. In a 1777 issue of Wesley's catalogs was the advertisement: "137 Thoughts on Slavery, *large* 1s, *small* 2d." (The title varies, as was often the case in Wesley's references to his own publications. The title remained unchanged, even though it sometimes appeared as *Thoughts on Slavery.*)

As was to be expected, *Thoughts upon Slavery* was both praised and condemned. There was "speedy and vindictive" opposition in Britain. In America, one author later claimed "it probably exerted a greater influence upon the public conscience than any book ever written, not excepting *Uncle Tom's Cabin,* for the reception of which it prepared the way."[14]

It must be kept in mind, when reading *Thoughts upon Slavery,* that John Wesley was revealing his social philosophy to the world. He was presenting his views, giving them his signet, his imprimatur. In short, he was placing his good name "on the line."

The Monthly Review gave unexpected praise to Wesley for *Thoughts upon Slavery:*

This pamphlet contains many facts on good authority, or as good as could be found, . . . and the writer has made many pertinent observations . . . which do honour to his humanity, the more so as the subject is treated in a liberal manner, without being debased by any peculiar tincture—which was perhaps to be apprehended.[15]

John Wesley was being recognized as a prophet—even by his critics.

Quite naturally, there were vituperative retorts. One reader of *The Monthly Review,* in the October, 1774, issue, a slaveholder, expressed his opinion of Wesley's *Thoughts upon Slavery.* The correspondent insisted he was kind to his slaves; furthermore Georgia law protected the slaves from unduly severe treatment. He went on, regarding that shocking avowal in Section III, subsection 11, where Wesley had declared, "One gentleman, when I was abroad, thought fit to roast his slave alive!" The reader had no doubt about the truth of the statement, but he had personally not heard of such treatment.

Wesley calmly replied, November 30, 1774, citing two advertisements from the *Williamsburg Gazette* and a newspaper in North Carolina, whereby a small reward was offered for each slave which had run away, brought back alive, but a considerably larger reward for "his head severed from his body." Wesley was giving his information from "a letter from Philadelphia" which was before him, dated May 23, 1774, and the letter was from Anthony Benezet.[16]

Thoughts upon Slavery was the perennial favorite of antislavery groups everywhere. As the next thirty years passed, at least thirteen new editions appeared in the United States.

Other Publications

Wesley was not content to let a single monograph tell the story. He took every possible opportunity, as in the scathing reference to slavery in his 1775 *A Calm Address to Our American Colonies.* The Americans insisted they would no longer be slaves. Wesley asked:

"Who then is a slave?" Look into America, and you may easily see. See that Negro, fainting under the load, bleeding under the lash! He is a slave. And is there "no difference" between him and his master? Yes; the one is screaming, "Murder! Slavery!" the other silently bleeds and dies!

"But wherein then consists the difference between liberty and slavery?" Herein: You and I, and the English in general, go where we will, and enjoy the fruit of our labours: This is liberty. The Negro does not: This is slavery.[17]

The year 1776 saw Wesley producing *A Seasonable Address To The More Serious Part Of The Inhabitants Of Great Britain*. The "Unhappy Contest" between Britain and America had only exacerbated the feelings of the two English-speaking peoples. He enumerates the failures and sins of both, reminding them the great monarchies "rose by virtue; but they fell by vice," and one obvious vice of Britain:

One principal sin of our nation is, the blood that we have shed in Asia, Africa, and America. Here I would beg your serious attention, while I observe, that however extensively pursued, and of long continuance, the African trade may be, it is nevertheless iniquitous from first to last. It is the price of blood! It is a trade of blood, and has stained our land with blood!

He then speaks of East India trade, even "though here is no leading into captivity" as in Africa, the result has been war and plunder. He says:

What millions have fallen by these means, as well as by artificial famine! O earth, cover not thou their blood! . . . O ye Governors of this great nation, would to God that ye had seen this, and timely done your utmost to separate those tares from the wheat of fair and honest trade![18]

Whether it was African slavery or East India exploitation, it was a sin.

In 1778, Wesley published his *A Serious Address To The People of England, With Regard To The State Of The Nation.*

He reminded them of the fallen state of affairs in many quarters, not the least unhappy situation was the infamous slave trade:

"Nay, but we have also lost our Negro trade." I would to God it may never be found more! that we may never more steal and sell our brethren like beasts; never murder them by thousands and tens of thousands! O may this worse than Mahometan, worse than Pagan, abomination, be removed from us for ever! Never was anything such a reproach to England since it was a nation, as the having any hand in this execrable traffic.[19]

Wesley's interest in African people continued, and he used many means to demonstrate his appreciation for their contribution to the general welfare and cultural uplift. Beginning with 1781 in the *Arminian Magazine*, Wesley published some nine extracts from *Poems* by "Miss Phillis Wheatley, a Negro."[20]

Captain Richard Williams, who lived "Near Truro, Cornwall," regarded himself a poet and sent his work to Wesley. "I think the lines on Slavery will do well! They are both sensible and poetical," wrote Wesley on November 9, 1783.[21] Unfortunately for Williams his verse did not see the light of day in the *Arminian Magazine*. Wesley, as is so often the practice of editors, sent the poetry to another. On December 10 Wesley informed Williams, "I have directed your lines to the editor of the *General Post*. Both he and Mr. Pine [Wesley's printer] will insert in their papers only what they believe will promote the sale of them."[22] Neither the *General Post* nor a Bristol newspaper saw fit to publish it (an old story with poets and would-be authors).

The *Arminian Magazine* for July and August of 1788 carried Wesley's "A summary View of the Slave Trade," a digest of an earlier work, demonstrating the gross inequality and brutishness of the system.

CHAPTER
IX

ABOLITION OF SLAVERY

*J*ohn Wesley made it clear that the sins of the world would be judged. He made it equally explicit that slaveholders, slave merchants, those who invested in slave property and others of the same ilk were all stained with the blood of those slaves and "covered with guilt for their heinous crime."[1] There was more. Not only did the general reading public know where Wesley stood on the matter of slavery, but *Thoughts upon Slavery*, among other things, put him in close contact with others who were deeply committed to the abolition of the slave trade.[2]

The reading of *Historical Account of Guinea* and *A Caution and Warning* by Benezet had been a revelation and blessing for Wesley. These, and other substantiating pamphlets, simply confirmed and documented what he had long stood for and felt. Now, there was a fellowship; rapport among those of kindred minds. These like-minded spirits supported one another. An important aggregation it was!

One question cannot be resisted, Why did it take so long for the several humanitarian organizations to appear in the eighteenth century? The slave trade had been flourishing since mid-fifteenth century.[3] Is this not the case in most reformations? It usually necessitates considerable time for the seers of God and humanity to appear.

Wesley did emerge as a social prophet, and at a juncture when other people of liberal inclination needed him. Not only had Wesley by this time become one of the best-known figures in Britain, apart from certain governmental personalities, but he was immensely popular. And this was not just among the Methodists. He had an organization whereby he could reach masses of people. He had his many preachers, the Conference, the Societies. He also had access to the printing presses of Britain.

There was an important addition: Wesley knew how to reach the public. He was a genius at it. He knew how to make people laugh, or perhaps smile, at themselves—about serious matters. He could cause people to see how unreasonable certain aspects of life were, and slavery was a case in point.

Wesley utilized his *Journal* for more than personal, private notations. That *Journal* appeared in print; it was read country-wide. He made full use of it. One example would be the entry for Monday, April 14, 1777:

I preached about noon at Warrington, and in the evening at Liverpool; where many large ships are now laid up in the docks, which had been employed for many years in buying or stealing poor Africans, and selling them in America for slaves. The men-butchers have now nothing to do at this laudable occupation. Since the American war broke out, there is no demand for human cattle. So the men of Africa, as well as Europe, may enjoy their native liberty.[4]

Thomas Clarkson

John Wesley was not alone in finding Benezet thrilling. Another was Thomas Clarkson—a man destined to play a leading role in the battle against slavery.

In 1785, Dr. Peckard, vice chancellor of Cambridge, proposed a Latin dissertation for senior bachelor of arts candidates of whom Clarkson was one. The assigned topic: *Anne liceat invitos in servitutem dare?* (Is it right to make slaves of others against their will?)

The previous year young Clarkson had won the prize for the best Latin dissertation, and, though unfamiliar with the topic, he enthusiastically began his research. He was determined to win a second time. He recalled the experience:

". . .when going by accident (says he) into a friend's house, I took up a newspaper, then lying on the table; one of the articles which attracted my notice, was an advertisement of Anthony Benezet's historical account of Guinea. I soon left my friend and his paper, and to lose no time, hastened to London to buy it. In this precious book I found almost all I wanted."[5]

And Thomas Clarkson became one of the champions in the pitched battle against slavery. It hardly needs to be said, young Clarkson won the first prize.

The Committee for Abolition

The Committee for the Abolition of the Slave Trade[6] was formed May 22, 1787. It was a significant day, and, thanks to the dedicated work of faithful Quakers and the inspired leadership of public figures such as Granville Sharp, chairman of the committee, it became an outstanding corpus of humanitarians engaged in a righteous cause.

From the Isle of Guernsey, Wesley wrote a long letter to Samuel Hoare, Esq., on August 18, 1787. This is a major document wherein Wesley outlined his views and concerns. Obviously, it is to the Abolition Committee.

Gentlemen,—A week or two ago I was favoured with a letter from Mr. Clarkson, informing me of his truly Christian design, to procure, if possible, an Act of Parliament for the abolition of slavery in our Plantations. I have long wished for the rolling away of this reproach from us, a reproach not only to religion, but to humanity itself. Especially when I read Mr. Benezet's tracts and what Mr. Sharp has written upon the subject. My friends in America are of the same mind. They have already emancipated several hundred of the poor negroes, and are setting more and more at liberty every day, as fast as they can do it with any tolerable convenience. This is making a little stand against this shocking abomination; but Mr. Clarkson's design strikes at the root of it. And if it can be put in execution will be a lasting honour to the British nation. It is with great satisfaction that I learn so many of you are determined to support him. But without doubt, you . . . [may] expect to meet with rough and violent opposition. For the slave-holders are a numerous, a wealthy, and consequently a very powerful body. And when you bring their craft into danger, do you not touch the apple of their eye? Will they not then raise all their forces against you and summon their friends from every side? And will they not employ hireling writers in abundance, who will treat you without either justice or mercy? But, I trust, Gentlemen, you will not be affright at this: no, not when some of your Friends turn against you: perhaps some who have made the warmest profession of goodwill, and the strongest promises of assisting you. I trust you will not be discouraged thereby; but rather more resolute and determined. I allow, with men this is impossible; but we know all things are possible with God! What little I can do to promote this excellent work I shall do with pleasure. I will print a large edition of the tract I wrote some years since, *Thoughts upon Slavery,* and send it (which I have an opportunity of doing once a month) to all my friends in Great Britain and Ireland; adding a few words in favour of your design, which I believe will have some weight with them. I commend you to Him who is able to carry you through all opposition and support you in all discouragements, and am, Gentlemen,

Your hearty well-wisher.[7]

There were more letters. Wesley was advancing in years, and his schedule was grueling. Nonetheless, his work did not abate.

Clarkson, the recording secretary, recalled the sitting of the Abolition Committee on August 27, 1787, "was distinguished by the receipt of letters from two celebrated persons . . . [the first was Brissot]. The second was from Mr. John Wesley, whose useful labours as a minister of the gospel are so well known to our countrymen."

The August, 1787, letter mentioned by Clarkson, from Wesley, written in London, is an epistle of common sense. An old man was giving wise counsel. The original letter must have been the communication to Samuel Hoare. Clarkson gave the following précis:

'Mr. Wesley informed the Committee of the great satisfaction which he also had experienced when he heard of their formation. He conceived that their design, while it would destroy the slave trade, would also strike at the root of the shocking abomination of slavery.'

Wesley then provided down-to-earth suggestions:

'He desired to forewarn them that they must expect difficulties and great opposition from those who were interested in the system, that they were a powerful body, and that they would raise all their forces when they perceived their craft to be in danger. They would employ hireling writers, who would have neither justice nor mercy. But the Committee were not to be dismayed by such treatment, nor even if some of those professing goodwill toward them should turn against them. As to himself, he would do all he could to promote the object of their institution. He would reprint a new large edition of his *Thoughts upon Slavery,* and circulate it among his friends in England and Ireland, to whom he would add a few words in favour of their design. And then he concluded in these words: "I commend you to Him who is able to carry you through all opposition and support you under all discouragements." '[8]

Clarkson had long held Wesley in high regard. He had said of Mr. Wesley:

In the year 1774, John Wesley, the celebrated divine, to whose pious labours the religious world will be long indebted, undertook the cause of the poor Africans. He had been in America, and had seen and pitied their hard condition. The work which he gave to the world in consequence, was entitled Thoughts on Slavery. Mr. Wesley had this great cause much at heart, and frequently recommended it to the support of those who attended his useful ministry.[9]

On October 11, 1787, Wesley wrote to Granville Sharp, from London. It is the communication from an expert in human affairs, repeating judicious pointers. It underscores Wesley's sense of reality: dealing with the slave monopoly would require infinite patience along with sagacity. He was a shrewd old campaigner:

Sir,—Ever since I heard of it first I felt a perfect detestation of the horrid Slave Trade, but more particularly since I had the pleasure of reading what you have published upon the subject. Therefore I cannot but do everything in my power to forward the glorious design of your Society. And it must be a comfortable thing to every man of humanity to observe the spirit with which you have hitherto gone on. Indeed, you cannot go on without more than common resolution, considering the opposition you have to encounter, all the opposition which can be made by men who are not encumbered with either honour, conscience, or humanity, and will rush on *per fasque ne fasque;* through every possible means, to secure their great goddess, Interest. Unless they are infatuated in this point also, they will spare no money to carry their cause; and this has the weight of a thousand arguments with the generality of men.

As though sufficient warning had not been given, Wesley continued with the pragmatic admonition:

And you may be assured these men will lay hold on and improve every possible objection against you. I have been afraid lest they should raise an objection from your manner of procuring information. To *hire* or to *pay* informers has a bad sound and might raise great, yea insurmountable prejudice aginst you. Is it not worth your consideration whether it would not be advisable to drop this mode entirely, and to be content with such information as you can procure by more honourable means?

Wesley concluded with more sound observations:

After all, I doubt the matter will turn upon this, 'Is the Slave Trade for the interest of the nation?' And here the multitude of sailors that perish therein will come to be considered. In all these difficulties what a comfort it is to consider (unfashionable as it is) that there is a God! Yea, and that (as little as men think of it!) He has still all power both in heaven and on earth! To Him I commend you and your glorious Cause; and am, sir,

Your affectionate servant.[10]

Thomas Clarkson said that Wesley wrote a second letter to the Abolition Committee, received on October 30, 1787. As Clarkson put it, the message from Wesley ran:

'he had now read the publications which the Committee had sent him, and that he took, if possible, a still deeper interest in their cause. He exhorted them to more than ordinary diligence and perseverance; to be prepared for opposition; to be cautious about the manner of procuring information and evidence, that no stain might fall upon their character; and to take care that the question should be argued as well upon consideration of interest as of humanity and justice; the former of which he feared, would have more weight than the latter: and he recommended them and their glorious concern, as before, to the protection of Him who was able to support them.'[11]

This digest of Wesley's missive points up the Committee's respect for Wesley's admonitions, and their appreciation for Wesley the man. A long-lasting relationship was established.

Years brought wisdom to John Wesley—practical, down-to-earth discernment. Lo, he is no longer the young Georgia clergyman who, for all his good intentions, could not understand many of his people. Nor could they, at that time, understand him. He is now the elder statesman, wise to the ways of the world,[12] wise to the ways of God. He likewise understood people. He saw through the contrived schemes. He comprehended the subtle, uncanny motives so often unobserved by the naive. He knew when people were lying. In spite of it all, he continued to reach out to a world parish, to the total human family. His was forever a gospel of hope. The vilest might be converted. Redemption was always possible!

It was John Stuart Mill who, thinking of British concern for emancipation of slaves, remarked "one person with a belief is a social power equal to ninety-nine who have only interests."[13] John Wesley would certainly fit such a pen portrait. He was a "social power."[14]

Wesley wrote Granville Sharp, from City Road, on November 14, 1787, offering comfort and support. It was not a pleasant conflict:

Sir,—It was from a real desire to promote in whatever way I could the excellent design which you have in hand that I mentioned to you (not to others) that report which is current in several places, particularly at Bristol. And I am glad I did mention it, because it is now in my power to justify the Society from the imputation.

He continued:

To bear the expenses of witnesses coming from distant parts is undoubtedly an act of justice, which is liable to no objection. I believe you judge right in supposing the other report was circulated, if not invented too, by those who leave no means untried to raise prejudice against the institution. These certainly will use every possible method to blacken your character. Every opportunity of clearing it will be gladly taken by, sir,
Your obedient servant.[15]

Wesley was obviously in the thick of the battle.

Wesley wrote to Thomas Funnell, on November 24, 1787, regarding the work of the Committee for the Abolition of the Slave Trade:

My Dear Brother,—Whatever assistance I can give those generous men who join to oppose that execrable trade I certainly shall give. I have printed a large edition of the *Thoughts on Slavery*, and dispersed them to every part of England. But there will be vehement opposition made, both by slave-merchants and slave-holders; and they are mighty men. But our comfort is, He that dwelleth on high is mightier.—I am
Your affectionate brother.[16]

Most people—Paul, Augustine, and Luther among them—repeat themselves in the various letters they write. Wesley was no exception. There is so much repetition that the letters become tedious. Nonetheless, these communications were not tedious to those who received them. Individual letters seldom are.

A letter was sent from Bristol to Henry Moore on March 14, 1790:

Dear Henry,—I have received the parcel by the coach. I quite approve of your sending the note to all our Assistants, and hope it will have good effect. I would do anything that is in my power toward the extirpation of that trade which is a scandal not only to Christianity but humanity.[17]

While the contents of Moore's parcel remain unknown, as well as the note sent by him to the Assistants, it can be safely assumed both had a relationship to the war against slavery. Maybe copies of *Thoughts upon Slavery* were to be sent with the note to the Assistants.

Wesley's Spiritual Children in America

Wesley made a number of references to the antislavery feelings and activities of the Methodists in America. He had good reason to do so.

As early as the April 24, 1780, Conference, meeting in Baltimore, under the leadership of Francis Asbury, Question 16 asked: *"Ought not this conference to require those travelling Preachers who hold slaves, to give promises, to set them free?"*

Thomas Haskins, in writing of the Conference, had the additional phrase "on pain of future exclusion." The answer in the *Minutes*: *"Yes."*

Question 17 asked:

Does this conference acknowledge that slavery is contrary to the laws of God, man, and nature, and hurtful to society, contrary to the dictates of conscience and pure religion, and doing that which we would not others should do to us and ours?—Do we pass our disapprobation on all our friends who keep slaves, and advise their freedom?[18]

Thomas Haskins, in his notations, says, "insist on their freedom," then added, "Shall we read the minutes in every society? And the thoughts of slave-keeping, which was approved last Conference, and tell the people they must have but one year more before we exclude them?"[19] Answer in the *Minutes,* "Yes."

The *Minutes* for 1783, in Question 10, asked: *"What shall be done with our local Preachers who hold slaves contrary to the laws which authorize their freedom in any of the United States?"*

The Answer: "We will try them another year. In the meantime let every Assistant deal faithfully and plainly with every one, and report to the next conference. It may be necessary to suspend them."

The Conference meeting in Virginia on April 30, 1784, and ending in Baltimore, May 28, 1784, in Question 12, asked: *"What shall we do with our friends that will buy and sell slaves?"*

The Answer: "If they buy with no other design than to hold them as slaves, and have been previously warned, they shall be expelled; and be permitted to sell on no condition."

Question 13: *"What shall we do with our local Preachers who will not emancipate their slaves in the states where the laws admit it?"*

Answer: "Try those in Virginia another year, and suspend the preachers in Maryland, Delaware, Pennsylvania, and New-Jersey."[20]

It was the Christmas Conference, meeting December 24, 1784–January 2, 1785, at Lovely Lane Meeting House in Baltimore that the Methodist Episcopal Church in America was born.[21] The slavery issue was clearly reflected in the 1785 *Discipline.* "Are there any

Directions to be given concerning the Negroes?" The rejoinder: "Let every Preacher, as often as possible, meet them in Class. And let the Assistant always appoint a proper *White Person* as their Leader. Let the Assistants also make a regular Return to the Conference, of the Number of Negroes in Society in their respective Circuits."

Next, the Conference made the assault: "What Methods can we take to extirpate Slavery?" The mandate was probably the most eloquent statement of a social concern that early American Methodism would make! The 1785 *Discipline* was categorical:

We are deeply conscious of the Impropriety of making new Terms of Communion for a religious Society already established, excepting on the most pressing Occasion: and such we esteem the Practice of holding our Fellow-Creatures in Slavery. We view it as contrary to the Golden Law of God on which hang all the Law and the Prophets, and the unalienable Rights of Mankind, as well as every Principle of the Revolution, to hold in deepest Debasement, in a more abject Slavery than is perhaps to be found in any Part of the World except America, so many Souls that are all capable of the Image of God.

We therefore think it our most bounden Duty, to take immediately some effectual Method to extirpate this Abomination from among us: And for that Purpose we add the following to the Rules of our Society: viz.

1. Every Member of our Society who has Slaves in his Possession, shall within twelve Months after Notice given him by the Assistant (which Notice the Assistants are required immediately and without Delay to give in their respective Circuits) legally execute and record an Instrument, whereby he emancipates and sets free every Slave in his Possession who is between the Ages of Forty and Forty-five immediately, or at farthest when they arrive at the Age of Forty-five:

And every Slave who is between the Ages of Twenty-five and Forty immediately, or at the farthest at the Expiration of five Years from the Date of the said Instrument:

And every Slave who is between the Ages of Twenty and Twenty-five immediately, or at farthest when they arrive at the Age of Thirty:

And every Slave under the Age of Twenty, as soon as they arrive at the Age of Twenty-five at farthest.

And every Infant born in Slavery after the above-mentioned Rules are complied with, immediately on its Birth.

2. Every Assistant shall keep a Journal, in which he shall regularly minute down the Names and Ages of all the Slaves belonging to all the Masters in his respective Circuit, and also the Date of every Instrument executed and recorded for the Manumission of the Slaves, with the Name of the Court, Book and Folio, in which the said Instruments respectively shall have been recorded: Which Journal shall be handed down in each Circuit to the succeeding Assistants.

3. In Consideration that these Rules form a new Term of Communion, every Person concerned, who will not comply with them, shall have Liberty quietly to withdraw himself from our Society within the twelve Months succeeding the Notice given aforesaid: Otherwise the Assistant shall exclude him in the Society.

4. No person so *voluntarily withdrawn,* or so *excluded,* shall ever partake of the Supper of the Lord with the Methodists, till he complies with the above-Regulations.

5. No Person holding Slaves shall, in future, be admitted into Society or to the Lord's Supper, till he previously complies with these Rules concerning Slavery.

N.B. These Rules are to affect the Members of our Society no farther than as they are consistent with the Laws of the States in which they reside.

And respecting our Brethren in *Virginia* that are concerned, and after due Consideration of their peculiar Circumstances, we allow them *two years* from the Notice given, to consider the Expedience of Compliance or Non-Compliance with these Rules.

The final question asked by the *Discipline,* "What shall be done with those who buy or sell Slaves, or give them away?" The answer, clear cut: "They are immediately to be expelled: unless they buy them on purpose to free them."[22]

American Methodists at the Christmas Conference made a valiant witness against slavery.[23] In the six months following the Conference, Dr. Thomas Coke engaged in a heroic war against slavery in Virginia, and North Carolina, concluding with a call, along with Asbury, on George Washington.[24] Alas, the subsequent Conference, held in Baltimore in June, 1785, thought it prudent to suspend the minute concerning slavery: it meant rejection and delay.

The *Minutes* for 1785 state:

> It is recommended to all our brethren to suspend the execution of the minute on slavery, till the deliberations of a future conference; and that an equal space of time be allowed all our members for consideration, when the minute shall be put in force.

There followed N.B. "We do hold in the deepest abhorrence, the practice of slavery; and shall not cease to seek its destruction by all wise and prudent means."

In 1743 John Wesley had composed *The Nature, Design, and General Rules of the United Societies.* For those desiring "to flee from the wrath to come" there were certain specific guidelines. "It is therefore expected of all who continue therein that they should evidence their desire of salvation." In the 1789 edition of the *Discipline,* the Americans, doubtless Thomas Coke's work, added: "The buying or selling of men, women, and children with an intention to enslave them."[25] The Revival, which had burned "like fire among the stubble" during those early years in Britain, was likewise burning in America. Slavery was an issue American Methodists had to face.[26] There were many long, painful failures and setbacks in the subsequent story.

An interesting communication was dispatched to Francis Asbury, on November 25, 1787, from John Wesley. It deals chiefly with the neglected Indians in North and South America, but there is a reference to Africans:

> My Dear Brother,—A glorious work, indeed, God has been working for several years and is still working in America. But one thing has often given me concern: God is visiting the progeny of Japhet (the English), who now *dwell in the tents of Shem,* according to the prophecy of Noah. Nay, He does
>
> > The servile progeny of Ham
> > Seize as the purchase of His blood.[27]

Wesley then wrote, expressing his urgent concern for the American Indians, how they have been abused and neglected. His prayer is that laborers will be sent "into His harvest." While the bulk of the letter centers on the plight of the Indians, Wesley did not forget the black people he met in South Carolina. A bond had been established.

The Final Letter

"I am now an old man, decayed from head to foot," the eighty-six-year-old John Wesley noted in his *Journal* on Friday, January 1, 1790. "My eyes are dim; my right hand shakes much; my mouth is hot and dry every morning; I have a lingering fever almost every day; my motion is weak and slow." He continued, "However, blessed be God, I do not slack my labour. I can preach and write still."[28] And work, and preach, and write he did!

On February 22, 1791, Wesley recorded in his diary "4.30 Prayed, Miss R[itchie] read *Gustavus*; 7.30 tea. . . ."[29] The following day, Wednesday, February 23, Wesley made his last diary entry: "4.45 Prayed, on business, read; 6.30 prayed, tea, conversed; chaise, read *Gustavus Vasa*. . . .[30] The book, read to Wesley by Miss Elizabeth Ritchie, was *The Interesting Narrative of the Life of Olaudah Equiano, or Gustavus Vassa*, written by himself 2 vols. (London: printed and sold for the author by T. Wilkins, No. 23, Aldermanbury). Wesley's name appears among the subscribers. Wesley was reading the autobiography, in his chaise on his way to Leatherhead, where he preached his last sermon.

Olaudah Equiano, renamed Gustavus Vassa, was born in Africa in 1745. He was taken by slave hunters and sold as a slave in Barbados. In 1757 his master sent him to England. It was on the voyage that the captain gave him the name of Gustavus Vassa, for the celebrated liberator of Sweden, Gustavus Vasa. He was baptized in St. Margaret's, Westminster, in 1759. He was in the British navy and served for a length of time in the Caribbean. The statement which caught Wesley's eye was "no black man's testimony is admitted in the West Indies against any white man's whatever."[31]

John Wesley, now eighty-seven years of age, within a week of his death, took his pen and in trembling handwriting composed his last letter. It was to William Wilberforce, who was engaged in the titanic struggle to abolish the slave trade, attempting to win a favorable vote in the House of Commons.

Balam, *February* 24, 1791

Dear Sir,—Unless the divine power has raised you up to be as *Athanasius contra mundum* [Athanasius against the world], I see not how you can go through your glorious enterprise in opposing that execrable villany, which is the scandal of religion, of England, and of human nature. Unless God has raised you up for this very thing, you will be worn out by the opposition of men and devils. But if God be for you, who can be against you? Are all of them together stronger than God? O be not weary of well doing! Go on, in the name of God and in the power of His might, till even American slavery (the vilest that ever saw the sun) shall vanish away before it.

Reading this morning a tract wrote by a poor African, I was particularly struck by that circumstance, that a man who has a black skin, being wronged or outraged by a white man, can have no redress; it being a *law* in all our Colonies that the *oath* of a black against a white goes for nothing. What villany is this!

That He who has guided you from your youth up may continue to strengthen you in this and all things is the prayer of, dear sir,

Your affectionate servant.[32]

With the writing of this—his concluding *magnum opus* of his thousands of written communications—Wesley, in effect, closed his long and fruitful ministry.

Wesley died at 10:00 A.M. on March 2, 1791, at his home in London. He was buried at City Road Chapel on March 9. William Wilberforce is the source of an illuminating docket: "John Wesley, his last words. Slave Trade."[33] Indeed, "In the same spirit in which the old crusader put off his armour the young crusader girded his on."

The abolition debate in the House of Commons began not long after Wesley's death. A few days prior to the debates, Wilberforce wrote, "May I look to Him for wisdom and strength and the power of persuasion. And ascribe to Him all the praise if I succeed; and if I fail, say from the heart, 'Thy will be done.' "[34]

On April 20, 1791, the House of Commons rejected Wilberforce's motion by 163 votes to 88. William Pitt, James Fox, and Edmund Burke spoke in favor of it. Wilberforce had to bring the issue before the House repeatedly. In 1807 there was a partial victory. It was not until August 1, 1838, that all technicalities were removed, and all slaves in the British Empire were emancipated. Victory!

The struggle had been long and arduous. There were many heroic prophets: the gentle Quakers who had worked assiduously in the Abolition Committee; of course such stalwarts as Sharp, Clarkson,[35] and Wilberforce.[36]

As the nineteenth century and the Victorian era drew to a close, the British looked at the Empire in retrospect, "The one imperial achievement that gave satisfaction to everybody was the ending of the slave trade."[37]

Perhaps the most remarkable part of the story is that a man, standing just five feet, three inches, and weighing one hundred twenty-two pounds, with "his ascetic chiseled features and dominating eyes,"[38] could stand up to his age and call Great Britain to repentance.

Victory over the slave trade had come at last, and a man named John Wesley played a significant role in the conflict, if not the triumph. An assessment has been made of John Wesley, "If we judge greatness by influence he was, barring Pitt, the greatest Englishman of his times.[39] How does history judge any individual? John Wesley's many-faceted career offers a variety of areas of concern and endeavor about God and humanity. Wesley will be remembered as one who was deeply committed to human welfare, especially the eradication of "that execrable sum of all villanies," the slave trade.

THOUGHTS

UPON

SLAVERY.

THE THIRD EDITION.

By *JOHN WESLEY*, A. M.

LONDON:
Printed by R. Hawes, (No. 34.) Lamb-Street,
Near *Spital-Square*. 1774.

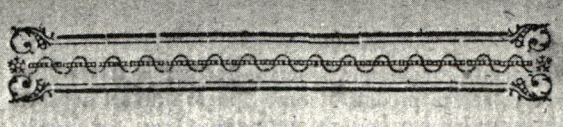

THOUGHTS

UPON

SLAVERY.

1. Y *Slavery* I mean, Domestic Slavery, or that of a Servant to a Master. A late ingenious Writer well observes, "The variety of forms in which Slavery appears, makes it almost impossible to convey a just notion of it, by way of Definition. There are however certain Properties which have accompanied Slavery in most places, whereby it is easily distinguished from that mild domestic *Service* which obtains in our Country*."

2. *Slavery* imports an obligation of perpetual Service, an obligation which only the consent of the Master can dissolve. Neither in some countries can the master himself dissolve it, without the consent of Judges appointed by the law. It generally gives the Master an arbitrary power of any correction, not affecting Life or Limb. Sometimes even these are exposed to his will: or protected only by a fine, or some flight punishment, too inconsiderable to restrain a Master of an harsh temper. It creates an incapacity of acquiring any thing, except for the Master's benefit. It allows the Master to alienate the Slave, in the same manner as his cows and horses. Lastly it descends in its full extent from parent to child, even to the last generation.

3. The beginning of this may be dated from the remotest period, of which we have an account in

B   history

---

* See Mr. *Hargrave's* Plea for *Somerset* the Negro

hiſtory. It commenced in the barbarous ſtate of Society, and in proceſs of time ſpread into all nations. It prevailed particularly among the *Jews*, the *Greeks*, the *Romans*, and the ancient *Germans*: And was tranſmitted by them to the various kingdoms and ſtates, which aroſe out of the *Roman* Empire. But after chriſtianity prevailed, it gradually fell into decline in almoſt all parts of *Europe*. This great change began in *Spain*, about the end of the Eighth Century: and was become general in moſt other kingdoms of *Europe*, before the middle of the Fourteenth.

4. From this time Slavery was nearly extinct, till the commencement of the Sixteenth Century, when the diſcovery of *America*, and of the Weſtern and Eaſtern coaſts of *Africa*, gave occaſion to the revival of it. It took its riſe from the *Portugeſe*, who to ſupply the *Spaniards* with men, to cultivate their new poſſeſſions in *America*, procured Negroes from *Africa*, whom they ſold for ſlaves to the *American* Spaniards. This began in the year 1508, when they imported the firſt Negroes into *Hiſpaniola*. In 1540, *Charles* the Fifth, then King of *Spain*, determined to put an end to *Negro-Slavery*: Giving poſitive orders, That all the Negro Slaves in the Spaniſh Dominions ſhould be ſet free. And this was accordingly done by *Lagaſca*, whom he he ſent and impowered to free them all, on condition of continuing to labour for their maſters. But ſoon after *Lagaſca* returned to *Spain*, Slavery returned and flouriſhed as before. Afterwards other nations, as they acquired poſſeſſions in *America*, followed the examples of the *Spaniards*; and Slavery has taken deep root in moſt of our *American* Colonies.

II. Such is the nature of Slavery: Such the beginning of Negroe Slavery in *America*. But ſome may deſire to know, what kind of country it is, from which the Negroes are brought? What ſort of men, of what temper and behaviour are they in their own country? And in what manner they are generally procured, carried to, and treated in *America*?

1. And

1. And first, What kind of country is that from whence they are brought? Is it so remarkably horrid, dreary and barren, that it is a kindness to deliver them out of it? I believe many have apprehended so: But it is an entire mistake, if we may give credit to those who have lived many years therein, and could have no motive to misrepresent it.

2. That part of *Africa* whence the Negroes are brought, commonly known by the name of *Guinea*, extends along the coast, in the whole, between three and four thousand miles. From the river *Senegal*, (Seventeen Degrees North of the Line) to Cape *Sierra Leona*, it contains seven hundred miles. Thence it runs Eastward about fifteen hundred miles, including the *Grain-Coast*, the *Ivory-Coast*, the *Gold-Coast*, and the *Slave-Coast*, with the large Kingdom of *Benin*. From thence it runs Southward, about twelve hundred miles, and contains the Kingdoms of *Congo* and *Angola*.

3. Concerning the first, the *Senegal* coast, Monf. *Brue*, who lived there sixteen years, after describing its fruitfulness near the sea, says, " The farther you go from the sea, the more fruitful and well-improved is the country, abounding in Pulse, Indian Corn, and various fruits. Here are vast meadows, which feed large herds of great and small cattle. And the villages which lie thick, shew the country is well peopled," And again; " I was surprized, to see the land so well cultivated; scarce a spot lay unimproved: The low lands divided by small canals, were all sowed with rice: The higher grounds were planted with Indian Corn, and Peas of different sorts. Their beef is excellent: poultry plenty, and very cheap, as are all the necessaries of life."

4. As to the *Grain* and *Ivory-Coast*, we learn from eye-witnesses, that the soil is in general fertile, producing abundance of rice and roots. Indigo and Cotton thrive without cultivation. Fish is in great plenty; the flocks and herds are numerous, and the trees loaden with fruit.

5. The

5. The *Gold-Coast* and *Slave-Coast*, all who have seen it agree, is exceeding fruitful and pleasant, producing vast quantities of rice and other grain, plenty of fruit and roots, palm-wine and oil, and fish in great abundance, with much tame and wild cattle. The very same account is given us of the soil and produce of the kingdoms of *Benin, Congo* and *Angola*. From all which it appears, That *Guinea* in general, is far from an horrid, dreary, barren country, is one of the most fruitful, as well as the most pleasant countries in the known world. It is said indeed to be unhealthy. And so it is to Strangers, but perfectly healthy to the native Inhabitants.

6. Such is the country from which the Negroes are brought. We come next to enquire, What sort of men they are, of what temper and behaviour, not in our Plantations, but in their native Country. And here likewise the surest way is to take our account from eye and ear-witnesses. Now those who have lived in the *Senegal* Country observe, it is inhabited by three Nations, the *Jalofs*, *Fulis* and *Mandingos*. The King of the *Jalofs* has under him several Ministers, who assist in the exercise of Justice. The Chief Justice goes in circuit through all his dominions, to hear complaints and determine controversies. And the Viceroy goes with him, to inspect the behaviour of the *Alkadi*, or governor of each village. The *Fulis* are governed by their Chief men, who rule with much moderation. Few of them will drink any thing stronger than water, being strict *Mahometans*. The Government is easy, because the people are of a quiet and good disposition; and so well instructed in what is right, that a man who wrongs another is the abomination of all. — They desire no more land than they use, which they cultivate with great care and industry: If any of them are known to be made slaves by the white men they all join to redeem them. They not only support all that are old, or blind, or lame among themselves; but have frequently supplied the necessaries of the *Mandingos*, when they were distrest by famine.

7. The

7. The *Mandingos*, says Monf. *Brue*, are right *Mahometans*, drinking neither wine nor brandy. They are induftrious and laborious, keeping their ground well cultivated, and breeding a good ftock of cattle. Every town has a Governor, and he appoints the labour of the people. The men work the ground defigned for corn; the women and girls, the rice-ground. He afterwards divides the corn and rice, among them: And decides all quarrels, if any arife. All the Mahometan Negroes conftantly go to public prayers thrice a day: there being a prieft in every village, who regularly calls them together: And it is furprizing to fee the modefty, attention and reverence which they obferve during their worfhip.— Thefe three Nations practife feveral trades; they have Smiths, Sadlers, Potters and Weavers. And they are very ingenious at their feveral occupations. Their Smiths not only make all the inftruments of iron, which they have occafion to ufe, but likewife work many things neatly in Gold and Silver. It is chiefly the women and children who weave fine cotton cloth, which they dye blue and black.

8. It was of thefe parts of *Guinea*, that Monf. *Adanfon*, Correfpondent of the Royal Academy of Sciences at *Paris*, from 1749, to 1753, gives the following account, both as to the country and people. "Which way foever I turned my eyes, I beheld a perfect image of pure nature: An agreeable folitude, bounded on every fide by a charming landfcape; the rural fituation of cottages, in the midft of trees; the eafe and quietnefs of the Negroes, reclined under the fhade of the fpreading foliage, with the fimplicity of their drefs and manners: The whole revived in my mind the idea of our firft parents, and I feemed to contemplate the world in i's primitive ftate. They are generally fpeaking, very good natured, fociable and obliging. I was not a little pleafed with my very firft reception, and it fully convinced me, that there ought to be a confiderable abatement made, in the accounts we have of the favage character of the *Africans*." He adds, " It is amazing that an

B 3   illiterate

illiterate people fhould reafon fo pertinently concerning the heavenly Bodies. There is no doubt, but
that with proper inftruments, they would become
excellent aftroncmers."

9. The inhabitants of the *Grain* and *Ivory Coaft*
are reprefented by thofe that deal with them, as fenfible, courteous, and the faireft traders on the coafts
of *Guinea*. They rarely drink to excefs: If any do
they are feverely punifhed by the King's order.
They are feldom troubled with war: If a difference
happen between two nations, they commonly end
the difpute amicably.

The inhabitants of the *Gold* and *Slave Coaft* likewife, when they are not artfully incenfed againft
each other, live in great union and friendfhip, being
generally well tempered, civil, tractable, and ready
to help any that need it. In particular, the natives
of the kingdom of *Whidah*, are civil, kind, and obliging to ftrangers. And they are the moft gentle-
man-like of all the Negroes, abounding in good manners toward each other, The inferiors pay the
utmoft refpect to their fuperiors: So Wives to their
hufbands, Children to their Parents. And they are
remarkably induftrious; all are conftantly employ'd;
the men in agriculture, the women in fpinning and
weaving cotton.

10. The *Gold* and *Slave Coafts* are divided into feveral diftricts, fome governed by Kings, others by the
principal men, who take care each of their own town
or village, and prevent or appeafe tumults. They
punifh Murder and Adultery feverely; very frequently with Death. Theft and Robbery are punifhed by a fine proportionable to the goods that were
taken.———All the natives of this coaft, though
heathens, believe there is One God, the Author of
them and all things. They appear likewife to have
a confufed apprehenfion of a future ftate. And
accordingly every town and village has a place of
public worfhip.—It is remarkable that they have no
Beggars among them; Such is the care of the chief
men,

men, in every city and village, to provide some eafy labour, even for the old and weak. Some are employed in blowing the Smith's bellows; others in preffing palm-oil; others in grinding of colours. If they are too weak even for this, they fell provifions in the Market.

11. The natives of the kingdom of *Benin* are a reafonable and good-natured people. They are fincere and inoffenfive, and do no injuftice either to one another or to ftrangers. They are eminently civil and courteous : If you make them a prefent, they endeavour to repay it double. And if they are trufted, till the fhip returns the next year, they are fure honeftly to pay the whole debt. Theft is punifhed among them, altho' not with the fame feverity as Murder. If a man and woman of any quality, are taken in adultery, they are certain to be put to death, and their bodies thrown on a dunghill, and left a prey to wild beafts. They are punctually juft and honeft in their dealings ; and are alfo very charitable : the King and the great Lords taking care to employ all that are capable of any work. And thofe that are utterly helplefs they keep for God's Sake ; fo that here alfo are no Beggars. The inhabitants of *Congo* and *Angola* are generally a quiet people. They difcover a good underftanding, and behave in a friendly manner to ftrangers, being of a mild temper and an affable carriage.—Upon the whole therefore the Negroes who inhabit the coaft of *Africa*, from the river *Senegal* to the Southern bounds of *Angola*, are fo far from being the ftupid, fenfelefs, brutifh, lazy barbarians, the fierce, cruel, perfidious Savages they have been defcribed, that on the contrary, they are reprefented by them who have no motive to flatter them, as remarkably fenfible, confidering the few advantages they have for improving their underftanding : As induftrious to the higheft degree, perhaps more fo than any other natives of fo warm a climate : As fair, juft and honeft in all their dealings, unlefs where White men have taught

them

them to be otherwise: And as far more mild, friendly and kind to Strangers, than any of our Forefathers were. Our Forefathers! Where shall we find at this day, among the fair-faced natives of *Europe*, a nation generally practising the Justice, Mercy, and Truth, which are found among these poor *Africans*? Suppose the preceding accounts are true, (which I see no reason or pretence to doubt of) and we may leave *England* and *France*, to seek genuine Honesty in *Benin, Congo*, or *Angola*.

III. We have now seen what kind of Country it is, from which the Negroes are brought : And what sort of men (even White-men being the Judges) they were in their own Country, Enquire we, Thirdly, In what manner are they generally procured, carried to, and treated in *America*.

1. *First*. In what manner are they procured? Part of them by fraud. Captains of Ships from time to time, have invited Negroes to come on board, and then carried them away. But far more have been procured by force. The Christians landing upon their coasts, seized as many as they found, men, women and children, and transported them to *America*. It was about 1551, that the *English* began trading to *Guinea* : At first, for Gold and Elephants teeth, but soon after, for Men. In 1556, Sir *John Hawkins* sailed with two ships to Cape *Verd*, where he sent eighty men on shore to catch Negroes. But the natives flying, they fell farther down, and there set the men on shore, " to burn their towns and take the inhabitants." But they met with such resistance, that they had seven men killed, and took but ten Negroes. So they went still farther down, till having taken enough, they proceeded to the *West-Indies* and sold them.

2. It was some time before the *Europeans* found a more compendious way of procuring *African* Slaves, by prevailing upon them to make war upon each other, and to sell their Prisoners. Till then they
seldom.

seldom had any wars : but were in gene.al quiet and peaceable. But the white men firſt taught them drunkenneſs and avarice, and then hired them to ſell one another. Nay, by this means, even their Kings are induced to ſell their own ſubjeċts. So Mr. *Moore* (Faċtor of the *African* Company in 1730) informs us, " When the King of *Barſalli* wants Goods or Brandy, he ſends to the *Engliſh* Governor at *James'* Fort, who immediately ſends a ſloop. Againſt the time it arrives, he plunders ſome of his neighbours towns, ſelling the people for the goods he wants. At other times he falls upon one of his own towns, and makes bold to ſell his own ſubjeċts." So Monſ. *Brue* ſays, " I wrote to the King (not the ſame) ," if he had a ſufficient number of ſlaves I would treat with him. He ſeized three hundred of his own people, and ſent word, he was ready to deliver them for the Goods." He adds, " Some of the natives are always ready" (when well paid) " to ſurprize and carry off their own countrymen. They come at night without noiſe, and if they find any lone cottage, ſurround it and carry off all the people." —*Barbot*, (another French Faċtor) ſays, " Many of the Slaves ſold by the Negroes are priſoners of war, or taken in the incurſions they make into their enemy's territories. Others are ſtolen. Abundance of little Blacks of both ſexes, are ſtolen away by their neighbours, when found abroad on the road, or in the woods, or elſe in the corn-fields, at the time of year when their parents keep them there all day to ſcare away the devouring birds." That their own parents ſell them, is utterly falſe : Whites not Blacks, are without natural affeċtion !

3. To ſet the manner wherein Negroes are procured in a yet ſtronger light, it will ſuffice to give an extraċt of two voyages to *Guinea* on this account. The firſt is taken verbatim from the original manuſcript of the Surgeon's Journal.

" Sestro, Dec. 29, 1724. No trade to-day, though many traders came on board. They informed us, that the people are gone to war within land,
and

and will bring prisoners enough in two or three days; in hopes of which we stay.

"The 30th. No trade yet: but our traders came on board to-day, and informed us the people had burnt four towns: So that to-morrow we expect slaves off.

" The 31st, Fair weather: but no trading yet. We see each night towns burning. But we hear many of the *Sestro* men are killed by the inland Negroes: So that we fear this war will be unsuccessful.

"The 2d. of January. Last night we saw a prodigious fire break out about eleven o'clock, and this morning see the town of *Sestro* burnt down to the ground." (It contained some hundred houses.) " So that we find their enemies are too hard for them at present, and consequently our trade spoiled here. Therefore about seven o'clock we weighed anchor, to proceed lower down."

4. The second Extract taken from the Journal of a Surgeon, who went from *New York* on the same trade, is as follows. " The Commander of the vessel sent to acquaint the King, that he wanted a cargo of slaves. The King promised to furnish him and, in order to it, set out, designing to surprize some town, and make all the people prisoners. Some time after, the King sent him word, he had not yet met with the desired success: Having attempted to break up two towns, but having been twice repulsed: But that he still hoped to procure the number of slaves. In this design he persisted, till he met his enemies in the field. A battle was fought, which lasted three days. And the engagement was so bloody, that four thousand five hundred men were slain upon the spot."————Such is the manner wherein the Negroes are procured! Thus the Christians preach the Gospel to the Heathens!

5. Thus they are *procured*. But in what numbers and in what manner are they carried to *America?*— Mr. *Anderson* in his history of Trade and Commerce, observes, " *England* supplies her American Colonies with Negro-slaves, amounting in number to about

about an hundred thousand every year." That is, so many are taken on board our ships; but at least ten thousand of them die in the voyage: About a fourth part more die at the different Islands, in what is called the Seasoning. So that at an average, in the passage and seasoning together, thirty thousand die: that is, properly are murdered. O Earth, O Sea, cover not thou their blood !

6. When they are brought down to the shore in order to be sold, our Surgeons thoroughly examine them, and that quite naked, women and men, without any distinction: Those that are approved are set on one side. In the mean time a burning iron, with the arms or name of the Company, lies in the fire, with which they are mark'd on the breast. Before they are put into the ships, their masters strip them of all they have on their backs: So that they come on board stark naked, women as well as men. It is common for several hundred of them to be put on board one vessel: where they are stowed together in as little room, as it is possible for them to be crowded. It is easy to suppose what a condition they must soon be in, between heat, thirst and stench of various kinds. So that it is no wonder, so many should die in the passage; but rather that any survive it.

7. When the vessels arrive at their destined port, the Negroes are again exposed naked, to the eyes of all that flock together, and the examination of their purchasers: Then they are separated to the plantations of their several Masters, to see each other no more. Here you may see Mothers hanging over their daughters, bedewing their naked breasts with tears, and daughters clinging to their parents, till the Whipper soon obliges them to part. And what can be more wretched than the condition they then enter upon ? Banished from their country, from their friends and relations for ever, from every comfort of life, they are reduced to a state scarce any way preferable to that of beasts of burden. In general a few roots, not of the nicest kind, usually yams or potatoes, are their food, and two rags, that neither screen
them

them from the heat of of the day, nor the cold of the night their covering. Their sleep is very short, their labour continual, and frequently above their strength; so that death sets many of them at liberty, before they have lived out half their days. The time they work in the *West Indies*, is from day-break to noon, and from two-o'clock till dark: During which time they are attended by overseers, who, if they think them dilatory, or think any thing not so well done as it should be, whip them most unmercifully, so that you may see their bodies long after wheal'd and scarred usually from the shoulders to the waist. And before they are suffered to go to their quarters, they have commonly something to do, as collecting herbage for the horses, or gathering fewel for the boilers. So that it is often past twelve before they can get home. Hence if their food is not prepared, they are some times called to labour again, before they can satisfy their hunger. And no excuse will avail. If they are not in the field immediately, they must expect to feel the lash. Did the Creator intend that the noblest Creatures in the visible world, should live such a life as this!

" Are *these* thy glorious works, Parent of Good? "

8 As to the Punishment inflicted on them, says Sir *Hans Sloan,* " they frequently geld them, or chop off half a foot: After they are whipped till they are raw all over, Some put pepper and salt upon them: Some drop melted wax upon their skin, Others cut off their ears, and constrain them to broil and eat them. For Rebellion," (that is, asserting their native Liberty, which they have as much right to as to the Air they breathe) " they fasten them down to the ground with crooked sticks on every limb, and then applying fire by degrees, to the feet and hands, they burn them gradually upward to the head."

9 But will not the laws made in the Plantations, prevent or redress all Cruelty and Oppression? We
will

will take but a few of those Laws for a specimen, and then let any man judge.

In order to rivet the chain of Slavery, the law of *Virginia* ordains, " That no slave shall be set free, upon any pretence whatever, except for some meritorious services, to be adjudged and allowed by the *Governor and Council*: And that where any slave shall be set free by his Owner, otherwise than is herein directed, the Church-wardens of the parish wherein such Negro shall reside for the space of one month are hereby authorized and required, to *take up and sell* the said Negro, by *public outcry.*"

Will not these Law-givers take effectual care, to prevent cruelty and Oppression?

The Law of *Jamaica* ordains, " Every slave that shall run away, and continue absent from his master twelve months, shall be *deemed rebellious* :" And by another law, " fifty pounds are allowed, to those who kill or bring in alive a *rebellious* slave." So their law treats these poor men with as little ceremony and consideration, as if they were merely brute beasts! But the innocent blood which is shed in consequence of such a detestable law, must call for vengeance on the murderous abetters and actors of such deliberate wickedness.

11. But the law of *Barbadoes* exceeds even this, " If any Negro under punishment, by his master, or his order, for running away, or any other crime or misdemeanor, shall suffer *in life or member, no person whatsoever shall be liable to any fine therefore.* But if any man, of WANTONNESS, or only of BLOODY-MINDEDNESS or CRUEL INTENTION, *wilfully kill* a negro of his own" (Now observe the severe punishment!) " He shall pay into the public treasury fifteen pounds sterling! And not be liable to any other punishment or forfeiture for the same!"

Nearly allied to this is that Law of *Virginia* : " After proclamation is issued against slaves that run away, it is lawful for any person whatsoever to KILL AND DESTROY such slaves, by SUCH WAYS AND MEANS AS HE SHALL THINK FIT.

C

We

We have seen already some of the ways and means which have been *thought fit* on such occasions. And many more might be mentioned. One Gentleman, when I was abroad, *thought fit* to roast his slave alive! But if the most natural act of " running away" from intolerable tyranny, deserves such relentless severity, what punishment have these *Lawmakers* to expect hereafter, on account of their own enormous offences?

IV. 1. This is the plain, un-aggravated matter of fact. Such is the manner wherein our *African* Slaves are procured: Such the manner wherein they are removed from their native land, and wherein they are treated in our Plantations. I would now enquire, Whether these things can be defended, on the principles of even Heathen Honesty? Whether they can be reconciled (setting the Bible out of the question) with any degree of either Justice or Mercy?

2. The grand plea is, " They are authorized by Law." But can Law, Human Law, change the nature of things? Can it turn Darkness into Light, or evil into good? By no means. Notwithstanding ten thousand Laws, right is right, and wrong is wrong still. There must still remain an essential difference between Justice and Injustice, Cruelty and Mercy. So that I still ask, Who can reconcile this treatment of the Negroes, first and last, with either Mercy or Justice?

Where is the Justice of inflicting the severest evils, on those that have done us no wrong? Of depriving those that never injured us in word or deed, of every comfort of life? Of tearing them from their native country, and depriving them of liberty itself? To which an *Angolan*, has the same natural right as an *Englishman*, and on which he sets as high a value? Yea where is the Justice of taking away the Lives of innocent, inoffensive men? Murdering thousands of them in their own land, by the hands of their own countrymen: Many Thousands, year after year,

on

on shipboard, and then casting them like dung into the sea! And tens of thousands in that cruel slavery, to which they are so unjustly reduced?

3. But waving, for the present, all other considerations, I strike at the root of this complicated villany. I absolutely deny all Slave-holding to be consistent with any degree of natural Justice.

I cannot place this in a clearer light, than that great ornament of his profession, Judge *Blackstone* has already done. Part of his words are as follows:

" The three origins of the Right of Slavery assigned by *Justinian*, are all built upon false foundations. 1. Slavery is said to arise from Captivity in War. The conqueror having a right to the life of his captive, if he spares that, has then a right to deal with them as he pleases. But this is untrue, if taken generally, That by the laws of nations, a man has a right to kill his enemy. He has only a right to kill him in particular cases, in cases of absolute necessity for self-defence. And it is plain, this absolute necessity did not subsist, since he did not kill him, but made him prisoner. War itself is justifiable only on principles of self-preservation. Therefore it gives us no right over prisoners, but to hinder their hurting us by confining them. Much less can it give a right to torture, or kill, or even enslave an enemy when the war is over. Since therefore the right of making our prisoners Slaves, depends on a supposed right of slaughter, that foundation failing, the consequence which is drawn from it must fail likewise."

" It is said Secondly, Slavery may begin, by one man's selling himself to another. And it is true, a man may sell himself to work for another: but he cannot sell himself to be a Slave, as above defined. Every sale implies an equivalent given to the Seller, in lieu of what he transfers to the Buyer. But what equivalent can be given for Life or Liberty? His Property likewise, with the very price which he seems

C 2   to

to receive, devolves *ipso facto* to his Master; the inſtant he becomes his ſlave : In this caſe therefore the buyer gives nothing, and the ſeller receives nothing. Of what validity then can a ſale be, which deſtroys the very principle upon which all ſales are founded ?"

"We are told, Thirdly, that men may be *born ſlaves*, by being the children of ſlaves. But this being built upon the two former rights muſt fall together with them, If neither Captivity, nor Contract can by the plain law of nature and reaſon, reduce the parent to a ſtate of ſlavery, much leſs can they reduce the offspring." It clearly follows, that all Slavery is as irreconcileable to Juſtice as to Mercy.

4. That Slave-holding is utterly inconſiſtent with Mercy, is almoſt too plain to need a proof. Indeed it is ſaid, "That theſe Negroes being priſoners of war, our Captains and Factors buy them, merely to ſave them from being put to death. And is not this Mercy?" I anſwer, 1. Did Sir *John Hawkins*, and many others, ſeize upon men, women and children, who were at peace in their own fields and houſes, merely to ſave them from death ? 2. Was it to ſave them from death, that they knock'd out the brains of thoſe they could not bring away ? 3. Who occaſioned and fomented thoſe wars, wherein theſe poor creatures were taken priſoners ? Who excited them by money, by drink, by every poſſible means, to fall upon one another ? Was it not themſelves ? They know in their own conſcience it was, if they have any conſcience left. But 4. To bring the matter to a ſhort iſſue. Can they ſay before GOD, That they ever took a ſingle voyage, or bought a ſingle Negro from this motive ? They cannot. They well know, to get money, not to ſave lives, was the whole and ſole ſpring of their Motions.

5. But if this manner of procuring and treating Negroes is not conſiſtent either with mercy or juſtice, yet there is a plea for it which every man of buſineſs will

will acknowledge to be quite sufficient. Fifty years ago, one meeting an eminent Statesman in the Lobby of the House of Commons, said, " You have been long talking about Justice and Equity. Pray which is this Bill? Equity or Justice?" He answered, very short, and plain, " D—n Justice: It is Necessity." Here also the Slave-holder fixes his foot: Here he rests the strength of his cause. " If it is not quite right, yet it *must* be so: There is an absolute *Necessity* for it. It is necessary we should procure Slaves: And when we have procured them, it is necessary to use them with severity, considering their stupidity, stubborness and wickedness."

I answer, You stumble at the threshold: I deny that villany is ever necessary. It is impossible that it should ever be necessary, for any reasonable creature to violate all the laws of Justice, Mercy, and Truth. No circumstances can make it necessary for a man to burst in sunder all the ties of humanity. It can never be necessary for a rational being to sink himself below a brute. A man can be under no necessity, of degrading himself into a wolf. The absurdity of the supposition is so glaring, that one would wonder any one could help seeing it.

6. This in general. But to be more particular, I ask, 1. What is necessary? And Secondly, To what end? It may be answered, " The whole method now used by the original purchasers of Negroes, is necessary to the furnishing our Colonies yearly with a hundred thousand Slaves." I grant this is necessary to that End. But how is that End necessary? How will you prove it necessary that one hundred, that *one* of those slaves should be procured?" " Why, it is necessary to my gaining an hundred thousand pounds." Perhaps so. But how is *this* necessary? It is very possible you might be both a better and a happier man, if you had not a quarter of it. I deny that your gaining one thousand is necessary, either to your present or eternal happiness. " But however you must allow, these slaves are necessary for the cultivation of our Islands: inasmuch as white

C 3　　　　men.

men are not able to labour in hot climates." I answer,
1. It were better that all those Islands should remain uncultivated for ever, yea, it were more desirable that they were altogether sunk in the depth of the sea, than that they should be cultivated at so high a price, as the violation of Justice, Mercy and Truth. But, Secondly, the supposition on which you ground your argument is false. For white men, even *English* men, are well able to labour in hot climates: provided they are temperate both in meat and drink, and that they inure themselves to it by degrees. I speak no more than I know by experience. It appears from the Thermometer, that the Summer Heat in *Georgia*, is frequently equal to that in *Barbadoes*, yea to that under the Line. And yet I and my Family (Eight in number) did employ all our spare time there, in felling of trees and clearing of ground, as hard labour as any Negro need be employed in. The *German* Family likewise, forty in number, were employed in all manner of labour. And this was so far from impairing our Health, that we all continued perfectly well, while the idle ones round about us, were swept away as with a pestilence. It is not true therefore that white men are not able to labour, even in hot climates, full as well as black. But if they were not, it would be better that none should labour there, that the work should be left undone, than that myriads of innocent men should be murdered, and myriads more dragged into the basest Slavery.

7. "But the furnishing us with Slaves is necessary, for the Trade, and Wealth, and Glory of our Nation:" Here are several mistakes. For 1. Wealth is not necessary to the Glory of any Nation; but Wisdom, Virtue, Justice, Mercy, Generosity, Public Spirit, Love of our Country. These are necessary to the real Glory of a Nation; but abundance of Wealth is not. Men of understanding allow, that the Glory of *England* was full as high, in Queen *Elizabeth's* time as it is now: Although our riches and trade were then as much smaller, as our Virtue

was

was greater. But, Secondly, it is not clear, that we should have either less Money or Trade, (only less of that detestable trade of Man-stealing) if there was not a Negro in all our Islands, or in all *English America.* It is demonstrable, White men, inured to it by degrees *can* work as well as them; And they *would* do it, were Negroes out of the way, and proper encouragement given them. However, Thirdly, I come back to the same point: Better no Trade, than trade procured by villany. It is far better to have no Wealth, than to gain Wealth at the expence of Virtue. Better is honest Poverty, than all the Riches bought by the tears, and sweat and blood of our fellow-creatures.

8. " However this be, it is necessary when we have Slaves, to use them with severity." What, to whip them for every petty offence, till they are all in gore blood ? To take that opportunity, of rubbing pepper and salt into their raw flesh ? To drop burning sealing-wax upon their skin ? To castrate them ? To cut off half their foot with an axe ? To hang them on gibbets, that they may die by inches, with heat, and hunger, and thirst ? To pin them down to the ground, and then burn them by degrees, from the feet, to the head ? To roast them alive ?—When did a Turk or a Heathen find it necessary to use a fellow-creature thus ?

I pray, to what end is this usage necessary ? " Why, to prevent their running away: And to keep them constantly to their labour, that they may not idle away their time. So miserably stupid is this race of men, yea, so stubborn and so wicked." Allowing them to be as stupid as you say, to whom is that stupidity owing ? Without question it lies altogether at the door of their inhuman Masters: Who give them no means, no opportunity of improving their understanding : And indeed leave them no motive, either from hope or fear, to attempt any such thing. They were no way remarkable for stupidity, while they remained in their own country : The inhabitants of *Africa* where they have equal motives
and

and equal means of improvement, are not inferior to the inhabitants of *Europe*: To some of them they are greatly superior. Impartially survey in their own country, the natives of *Benin*, and the natives of *Lapland*. Compare, (setting prejudice aside) the *Samoeids* and the *Angolans*. And on which side does the advantage lie, in point of understanding? Certainly the *African* is in no respect inferior to the *European*. Their stupidity therefore in our plantations is not natural; otherwise than it is the natural effect of their Condition. Consequently it is not their fault, but *Your's*: You must answer for it, before GOD and Man.

9. " But their Stupidity is not the only reason of our treating them with severity. For it is hard to say, which is the greatest, This or their Stubbornness and Wickedness."——It may be so: But do not these as well as the other, lie at *your* door? Are not Stubbornness, Cunning, Pilfering, and divers other vices, the natural, necessary fruits of Slavery? Is not this an observation which has been made, in every age and nation?——And what means have you used to remove this stubbornness? Have you tried what Mildness and Gentleness would do? I knew one that did: that had prudence and patience to make the experiment: Mr. *Hugh Bryan*, who then lived on the borders of *South Carolina*. And what was the effect? Why, that all his Negroes (And he had no small number of them) loved and reverenced him as a Father, and chearfully obeyed him out of love. Yea, they were more afraid of a frown from *him*, than of many blows from an overseer. And what pains have *you* taken, what method have *you* used, to reclaim them from their wickedness? Have you carefully taught them,

" That there is a GOD, a wise, powerful, merciful Being, the Creator and Governor of Heaven and Earth? That he has appointed a day wherein he will judge the world, will take an account of all our thoughts, words and actions? That in that day he will reward every child of man according to his works.

works: That "then the righteous shall inherit the kingdom prepared for them from the foundation of the world: And the wicked shall be cast into everlasting fire, prepared for the devil and his angels." If you have not done this, if you have taken no pains or thought about the matter, can you wonder at their wickedness? What wonder, if they should cut your throat? And if they did, whom could you thank for it but yourself? You first acted the villain in making them slaves, (whether you stole them or bought them.) You kept them stupid and wicked, by cutting them off from all opportunities of improving either in Knowledge or Virtue: And now you assign their want of Wisdom and Goodness as the reason for using them worse than brute beasts!

V. 1. It remains only to make a little application of the preceding observations.—But to whom should that application be made? That may bear a question. Should we address ourselves to the Public at large? What effect can this have? It may inflame the world against the guilty, but is not likely to remove that guilt. Should we appeal to the *English* nation in general? This also is striking wide; And is never likely to procure any redress for the sore evil we complain of.—As little would it in all probability avail, to apply to the Parliament. So many things, which *seem* of greater importance lie before them that they are not likely to attend to this. I therefore add a few words to those who are more immediately concerned, whether Captains, Merchants or Planters.

2. And, first, to the Captains employed in this trade. Most of *You* know, the country of *Guinea*: Several parts of it at least, between the River *Senegal* and the kingdom of *Angola*. Perhaps now, by *your* means, part of it is become a dreary uncultivated wilderness, the inhabitants being all murdered or carried away; so that there are none left to till the ground. But you well know, how populous, how fruitful, how pleasant it was a few years ago. You know the people were not stupid, not wanting in

sense

senfe, confidering the few means of improvement they enjoyed. Neither did you find them favage, fierce, cruel, treacherous, or unkind to strangers. On the contrary, they were in moſt parts, a fenfible and ingenious people. They were kind and friend-ly, courteous and obliging, and remarkably fair and juſt in their dealings. Such are the men whom you hire their own country-men; to tear away from this lovely country ; part by ſtealth, part by force, part made captive in thoſe wars, which you raiſe or foment on purpoſe. You have ſeen them torn away, Children from their Parents, Parents from their Children : Huſbands from their Wives, Wives from their beloved Huſbands, Brethren and Siſters from each other. You have dragged them who had never done you any wrong, perhaps in chains, from their native ſhore. You have forced them into your ſhips like an herd of ſwine, them who had ſouls immor-tal as your own : (Only ſome of them leaped into the ſea, and refolutely ſtayed under water, till they could ſuffer no more from you. You have ſtowed them together as cloſe as ever they could lie, with-out any regard either to decency or convenience. And when many of them had been poiſoned by foul air, or had funk under various hardſhips, you have ſeen their remains delivered to the deep, till the ſea ſhould give up his dead. You have carried the fur-vivors into the vileſt ſlavery, never to end but with life : Such Slavery as is not found among the Turks at *Algiers*, no nor among the Heathens in *America*,

3. May I ſpeak plainly to you ? I muſt. Love conſtrains me : Love to *You*, as well as to thoſe you are concerned with.

Is there a GOD ? You know there is. Is He a Juſt GOD ? Then there muſt be a ſtate of Retribu-tion : A ſtate wherein the Juſt GOD will reward every man according to his works. Then what reward will he render to *You ?* O think betimes ! Before you drop into eternity ! Think now, *He ſhall have Judgement without mercy that hath ſhewed no mercy.*

Are

Are you a *man*? Then you should have an *human* heart. But have you indeed? What is your heart made of? Is there no such principle as Compassion there? Do you never *feel* another's pain? Have you no Sympathy? No sense of human woe? No pity for the miserable? When you saw the flowing eyes, the heaving breasts, or the bleeding sides and tortured limbs of your fellow-creatures, was you a stone, or a brute? Did you look upon them with the eyes of a tiger? When you squeezed the agonizing creatures down in the ship, or when you threw their poor mangled remains into the sea, had you no relenting? Did not one tear drop from your eye, one sigh escape from your breast? Do you feel no relenting *now*? If you do not, you must go on, till the measure of your iniquities is full. Then will the Great GOD deal with *You*, as you have dealt with *them*, and require all their blood at your hands. And at that day it shall be more tolerable for Sodom and Gomorrah, than for *you!* But if your heart does relent, though in a small degree, know it is a call from the GOD of Love. And to-day, if you will hear his voice, harden not your heart. To-day resolve, GOD being your helper, to escape for your life. Regard not money! All that a Man hath will he give for his Life! Whatever you lose, lose not your soul: nothing can countervail that loss. Immediately quit the horrid trade: At all events, be an honest man.

4. This equally concerns every Merchant, who is engaged in the Slave-trade. It is *You* that induce the *African* villain to sell his countrymen; and in order thereto, to steal, rob, murder men, women and children without number: By enabling the *English* Villain to pay him for so doing; whom you over-pay for his execrable labour. It is *your* money, that is the spring of all, that impowers him to go on: So that whatever he or the *African* does in this matter, is all *your* act and deed. And is your conscience quite reconciled to this? Does it never reproach you

at all? Has gold entirely blinded your eyes, and stupified your heart? Can you see, can you *feel* no harm therein? Is it doing as you would be done to? Make the case your own. "Master, said a slave at *Liverpool* to the Merchant that owned him) " what if some of my countrymen were to come here, and take away my Mistress, and Master Tommy and Master Billy and carry them into our country, and make them slaves, how would you like it?" His answer was worthy of a man: "I will never buy a slave more while I live." O let his resolution be Your's! Have no more any part in this detestable business. Instantly leave it to those unfeeling wretches, "Who laugh at human nature and compassion! Be *you* a man! Not a wolf, a devourer of the human species! Be merciful, that you may obtain mercy!

5. And this equally concerns every Gentleman that has an estate in our *American* Plantations: Yea all Slave-holders of whatever rank and degree: seeing *Men-buyers* are exactly on a level with *Men-stealers*. Indeed you say, "I pay honestly for my goods: and I am not concerned to know how they are come by: Nay but you are: You are deeply concerned to know they are honestly come by. Otherwise you are partaker with a thief, and are not a jot honester than Him. But you know, they are not honestly come by: You know they are procured by means, nothing near so innocent as picking of pockets, house-breaking, or robbery upon the high-way. You know they are procured by a deliberate series of more complicated villany, (of fraud, robbery and murder) than was ever practised either by Mahometans or Pagans: in particular by murders, of all kinds; by the blood of the innocent poured upon the ground like water. Now it is *your* money that pays the Merchant, and thro' him the Captain, and the *African* Butchers. *You* therefore are guilty, yea principally guilty, of all these frauds, robberies and murders. You are the spring that puts all the rest in motion: they would not stir a step without *you*:

Therefore

Therefore the blood of all these wretches, who die before their time, whether in their country, or elsewhere lies upon *your* head. *The blood of thy brother*, (for, whether thou wilt believe it or no, such he is in the fight of Him that made him) *crieth against thee from the earth*, from the ship, and from the waters. O, whatever it costs, put a stop to its cry before it be too late: Instantly, at any price, were it the half of your goods, deliver thyself from blood-guiltiness! Thy hands, thy bed, thy furniture, thy house, thy lands are at present stained with blood. Surely it is enough; accumulate no more guilt; spill no more the blood of the innocent! Do not hire another to shed blood: Do not pay him for doing it! Whether you are a Christian or no, shew yourself a man! be not more savage than a lion or a bear!

6. Perhaps you will say, " I do not *buy* any Negroes: I only *use* those left me by my Father." So far is well: but is it enough to satisfy your own conscience? Had your Father, have you, has any man living, a right to use another as a slave? It cannot be, even setting Revelation aside. It cannot be, that either War, or Contract, can give any man such a property in another as he has in his sheep and oxen. Much less is it possible, that any child of man, should ever be *born a slave*. Liberty is the right of every human creature, as soon as he breathes the vital air. And no human law can deprive him of that right, which he derives from the law of nature.

If therefore you have any regard to Justice, (to say nothing of Mercy, nor the revealed Law of GOD) render unto all their due. Give Liberty to whom Liberty is due, that is to every child of man, to every partaker of human nature. Let none serve you but by his own act and deed, by his own voluntary Choice. Away with all whips, all chains, all compulsion! Be gentle toward all men. And see that you invariably do unto every one, as you would he should do unto *You*.

D   O

7. O thou GOD of Love, thou who art loving to every man, and whose mercy is over all thy works: Thou who art the Father of the Spirits of all flesh, and who art rich in mercy unto all: Thou who hast mingled of one blood, all the nations upon earth: Have compassion upon these outcasts of men, who are trodden down as dung upon the earth! Arise and help these that have no helper, whose blood is spilt upon the ground like water! Are not these also the work of thine own hands, the purchase of thy Son's blood? Stir them up to cry unto thee in the land of their captivity; and let their complaint come up before thee; let it enter into thy ears! Make even those that lead them away captive to pity them, and turn their captivity as the rivers in the South. O burst thou all their chains in sunder; more especially the chains of their sins: Thou, Saviour of all, make them free, that they may be free indeed!

> The servile progeny of *Ham*
>   Seize as the purchase of thy blood!
> Let all the Heathens know thy name:
>   From idols to the living GOD
> The dark *Americans* convert,
>   And shine in every pagan heart!

FINIS.

NOTES

PROLOGUE

1. See James Morris, *Heaven's Command: An Imperial Progress* (New York: Harcourt Brace Jovanovich, 1973), p. 33.

2. James Boswell, *The Life of Samuel Johnson L.L.D.* (New York: Random House, The Modern Library, n.d.), p. 749.

3. Morris, *Heaven's Command*, pp. 34-35.

4. Ibid.

5. Ibid, p. 35.

6. Ibid., p. 36. Chains and whips were taken to the school yard and buried, as the song was sung rather like a dirge.

7. J. T.McNeill, *Makers of Christianity* (New York: Henry Holt & Co., 1935), vol. 2, p. 247, states: "He [Wesley] began his real career when he preached in a brickyard beside Bristol to three thousand sooty miners, from the text: 'The spirit of the Lord is upon me, because he hath anointed me to preach the gospel to the poor.' It was the beginning of a national, indeed a world-wide, mission to the forgotten man." To the point is another evaluation: "The Wesleyan Revival is an outstanding illustration of the efficacy of the combined force of religion and ethics in locating anew the fundamental values of life, and in realizing them in the activities and experiences of the common people. The ethical ideal with a religious motivation is an old formula, but its restatement in terms consonant with current thought and conditions might prove 'a very present help' in our own troublous days," Kathleen Walker MacArthur, *The Economic Ethics of John Wesley* (New York: Abingdon Press, 1936), p. 12.

Chapter 1 Slavery

1. David Brion Davis, *Slavery and Human Progress* (New York: Oxford University Press, 1984), p. 33.

2. See Augustine, *The City of God*, Book 19, chapters 14-16. Also Lester B. Scherer, *Slavery and the Churches in Early America, 1619–1819* (Grand Rapids: Wm. B. Eerdmans Publishing Co., 1975), p. 15. Also see Warren Thomas Smith, *Augustine: His Life and Thought* (Atlanta, Ga.: John Knox Press, 1980), pp. 149-50.

3. Anthony Benezet, *Some Historical Account of Guinea* (Philadelphia: Printed by Joseph Crukshank, 1771), p. 41. Benezet's importance will be increasingly evident.

4. David Brion Davis, *The Problem of Slavery in the Age of Revolution, 1770–1823* (Ithaca: Cornell University Press, 1975), p. 41.

5. Davis, *Slavery and Human Progress*, p. 65.

6. In addition to works already cited, see John Hope Franklin, *From Slavery to Freedom: A History of the Negro Americans*, (New York: Alfred A. Knopf, 1967), chapter IV, "The Slave Trade," pp. 42-59. Also see Elizabeth Donnan, ed., *Documents Illustrative of the History of the Slave Trade to America*, 4 vols. (New York: Octagon Books, 1965); Kenneth Stampp, *The Peculiar Institution* (New York: Alfred A. Knopf, 1956); David Brion Davis, *The Problem of Slavery in Western Culture* (Ithaca: Cornell University Press, 1966); Lerone Bennett, Jr., *Before the Mayflower: A History of the Negro in America, 1619–1664*, rev. ed. (New York: Penguin Books, 1966). Also see related

studies: Albert J. Raboteau, *Slave Religion: The Invisible Institution in the Antebellum South* (New York: Oxford University Press, 1978); Winthrop S. Hudson, "The American Context as an Area for Research in Black Church Studies," *Church History*, 52 (June 1983), pp. 157-71.

7. Benezet, *Some Historical Account of Guinea*, pp. 52-53.

8. Ibid., p. 55.

9. See Robert William Fogel and Stanley L. Engerman, *Time on the Cross: The Economics of American Negro Slavery* (Boston: Little, Brown & Co., 1974), vol. I, p. 16.

10. Davis, *The Problem of Slavery in the Age of Revolution*, p. 52.

11. Bennett, *Before the Mayflower*, p. 13.

12. Ibid., pp. 3-28.

13. Benezet, *Some Historical Account of Guinea*, p. 121 ff.

14. Ibid., p. 126

15. Ibid., p. 117.

16. Ibid., p. 94.

17. Ibid., pp. 136-37.

18. See Franklin, *From Slavery to Freedom*, p. 59.

19. See Bennett, *Before the Mayflower*, p. 360. See Franklin, *From Slavery to Freedom*, pp. 46-47.

20. Bennett, *Before the Mayflower*, p. 361.

21. Ibid.

22. See Evarts B. Greene and Virginia D. Harrington, *American Population Before the Federal Census of 1790* (New York: Columbia University Press, 1932), p. 67. Also see Lorenzo Johnston Greene, *The Negro in Colonial New England, 1620–1776* (New York: Columbia University Press, 1942), pp. 74, 76. For helpful demographics of black population see Edwin S. Gaustad, *Historical Atlas of Religion in America*, rev. ed. (New York: Harper & Row, 1976), pp. 154-58.

Chapter II John Wesley and His Family

1. For a splendid overview of the Wesley family, see Maldwin Edwards, *Family Circle: A Study of the Epworth Household in Relation to John and Charles Wesley* (London: Epworth Press, 1949).

2. *The Journal of the Rev. Charles Wesley, M.A.* (London: Wesleyan Methodist Book-Room, [1849] n.d.), I, xxx.

3. See Dr. Coke and Mr. Moore, *The Life of the Rev. John Wesley, A.M.*, 2nd ed. (London: G. Paramore, 1792), p. 93.

4. See L. Tyerman, *The Life and Times of the Rev. John Wesley, M.A., Founder of the Methodists* (London: Hodder & Stoughton, MDCCCLXXV), I, 391.

5. See Richard P. Heitzenrater, "The Oxford Diaries and the First Rise of Methodism" in *Methodist History*, July 1974, XII, 110-35.

6. Nehemiah Curnock, ed., *The Journal of the Rev. John Wesley, A.M.* (London: Epworth Press, 1938), I, 109.

7. Biographical studies of the Wesleys abound. A popular work is Stanley Ayling, *John Wesley* (Nashville: Abingdon Press, 1981). Of a more technical nature, Richard P. Heitzenrater, *The Elusive Mr. Wesley* (Nashville: Abingdon Press, 1984), vol. 1, *John Wesley His Own Biographer;* vol. 2, *John Wesley as Seen by Contemporaries and Biographers*. Albert C. Outler, ed., *John Wesley* (New York: Oxford University Press, 1964) is valuable in interpreting John Wesley.

Chapter III Georgia: The Wesleys Meet Slavery

1. *The Narrative of the Expedition of Hernando De Soto, By the Gentleman of Elvas,* quoted in Spencer B. King., Jr., *Georgia Voices a Documentary History to 1872* (Athens: University of Georgia Press, 1966), p. 1.

2. Patrick Tailfer and others, *A True and Historical Narrative of the Colony of Georgia, with Comments by the Earl of Egmont.* Clarence L. Ver Steeg, ed. (Athens: University of Georgia Press, 1960), p. 24.

3. Frank Baker, *From Wesley to Asbury: Studies in Early American Methodism* (Durham, N.C.: Duke University Press, 1970), pp. 3 ff.

4. Tailfer, *A True and Historical Narrative,* p. 34.

5. Ibid., p. 39, see note 18.

6. See B. H. Fant, "The Labor Policy of the Trustees for Establishing the Colony of Georgia in America," in *The Georgia Historical Quarterly,* March 1932, XVI, 1.

7. For *A Brief Account of the Establishment of a Colony of Georgia Under General James Oglethorpe, February 1, 1733,* see King, p. 12.

8. Frank Baker, ed., *The Oxford Edition of the Works of John Wesley,* vol. 25, *Letters I, 1721–1739* (Oxford: Clarendon Press, 1980), p. 435.

9. Ibid., p. 436.

10. Ibid., pp. 439-41.

11. *The Diary of Viscount Perceval Afterwards First Earl of Egmont* (London: 1920, 1923), II, 196.

12. J. Wesley, *Journal,* I, 112-13, Tuesday, October 21.

13. Ibid., p. 123.

14. Ibid., pp. 145-49.

15. C. Wesley, *Journal,* I, 1 [4].

16. Ibid., p. 5, dated Sunday, March 21, 1736.

17. Ibid., pp. 35-36.

18. Ibid., p. 36.

19. Ibid., pp. 36-37. Also see Frank Baker, "The Origins, Character, and Influence of John Wesley's Thoughts upon Slavery," in *Methodist History,* vol. XXII, January 1984, p. 76.

20. Quoted in Egmont *Diary,* II:313-14, cited in Frank Baker, *John Wesley and the Church of England* (Nashville: Abingdon Press, 1970), pp. 43, 355.

21. C. Wesley, *Journal,* I, pp. 68-69.

22. Franz Hilderbrandt, Oliver A. Beckerlegge, eds., *The Oxford Edition of the Works of John Wesley,* vol. 7, *A Collection of Hymns for the Use of the People Called Methodists* (Oxford: Clarendon Press, 1983), hymn # 432, p. 609.

23. J. Wesley, *Journal,* I, pp. 254-55.

24. Ibid., p. 255.

25. Ibid., p. 260. Also see Baker, "The Origins, Character, and Influence of John Wesley's Thoughts upon Slavery," p. 75.

26. J. Wesley, *Journal,* I, p. 348.

27. Ibid.

28. Ibid., pp. 349-50. Also see Warren Thomas Smith, "Sketches of Early Black Methodists," in *The Journal Of The Interdenominational Theological Center,* Fall 1981, IX, 1-18.

29. J. Wesley, *Journal,* I, p. 350.

30. Ibid., pp. 350-51.

31. Ibid., p. 351.

32. Ibid., p. 352, see diary. (Brian is later referred to as Bryan in *Thoughts upon Slavery.*)

33. Ibid., p. 352.

34. Ibid., pp. 352-53.

35. Ibid., p., 400.

36. See Frank Baker, "John Wesley's Last Visit to Charleston," in *South Carolina Historical Magazine,* October 1977, pp. 265-71.

37. J. Wesley, *Journal,* I, p. 413.

38. Ibid., I, pp. 421-22. See note 2, p. 422. There is a possibility Wesley did not intend for this statement to be made public.

39. J. Wesley, *Journal,* I, p. 435. See Lucius C. Matlack, *The History of American Slavery and Methodism from 1780 to 1849* (Freeport, N.Y.: Books for Libraries Press [1849], 1971), pp. 9-27.

40. John Telford, ed., *The Letters of the Rev. John Wesley, A.M.* (London: The Epworth Press, 1931), VIII, p. 17.

41. Ralph Betts Flanders, *Plantation Slavery in Georgia* (Cos Cob, Conn.: John E. Edwards, 1967), p. 13. Also Betty Wood, *Slavery in Colonial Georgia, 1730–1775* (Athens: University of Georgia Press, 1984).

42. Fant, "The Labor Policy," p. 7.

43. Ibid.

44. Robert Vaux, *Memoirs of the Life of Anthony Benezet* (New York: Burt Franklin, 1817), p. 44. Note the line "who laugh at human nature and compassion . . ." Wesley will repeat it in *Thoughts upon Slavery,* Section V. subsection 4.

45. *George Whitefield's Journals* (London: The Banner of Truth Trust, 1960), p. 157, entry for Friday, June 2, 1738. Also see Stuart C. Henry, *George Whitefield, Wayfaring Witness* (New York: Abingdon Press, 1957).

46. See Henry, p. 116. Also see William E. Phipps, "John Wesley on Slavery," in *Quarterly Review,* Summer 1981, vol. I, pp. 24-25. Also see Albert D. Belden, *George Whitefield: The Awakener* (New York: The Macmillan Co., 1953), pp. 85-88.

47. See Warren Thomas Smith, *Preludes: Georgia, Methodism, the American Revolution* (Atlanta: Methodist Administrative Services, 1976), pp. 6-16. Also Warren Thomas Smith, "The Wesleys in Georgia: An Evaluation," in *The Journal Of The Interdenominational Theological Center,* Spring 1979, vol. VI. Regarding Jonathan Edwards, see Greene, p. 356.

Chapter IV The Wesleys in England: 1738–1757

1. See Warren Thomas Smith, "Spiritual Quests of the Wesleys," in *Circuit Rider,* June 1983, pp. 15-16.

2. C. Wesley, *Journal,* I, pp. 90-95.

3. Hildebrandt and Beckerlegge, *Works of John Wesley,* vol. 7, hymn # 29, pp. 116-17.

4. Ibid., vol. 7, hymn # 1, pp. 79-81.

5. J. Wesley, *Journal,* I, pp. 465-77.

6. C. Wesley, *Journal,* I, p. 120.

7. Hildebrandt and Beckerlegge, *Works of John Wesley,* vol. 7, p. 107.

8. C. Wesley, *Journal,* I, pp. 120-23.

9. J. Wesley, *Journal,* II, p. 362.

10. John Wesley, M.A., *Explanatory Notes upon the New Testament* (London: Printed by William Bowyer, MDCCLV), p. 558.

11. J. Wesley, *Journal*, IV, p. 125.

12. Ibid., IV, p. 149. Davies continued, "Sundry of them lodged all night in my kitchen . . . at two or three in the morning, a torrent of sacred psalmody has poured into my chamber."

13. Ibid., IV, pp. 194-95.

Chapter V Wesleyan Witness in the Caribbean

1. See Warren Thomas Smith, "Thomas Coke and the West Indies," in *Methodist History*, October 1964, vol. III, pp. 1-11.

2. Thomas Coke, *A History of the West Indies* (Liverpool: Nuttall, Fisher, and Dixon, 1810), II, pp. 426-27.

3. See Gerald R. Cragg, ed., *The Oxford Edition Of The Works Of John Wesley*, vol. 11, *The Appeals to Men of Reason and Religion and Certain Related Open Letters* (Oxford: Clarendon Press, 1975).

4. See Frank Baker, "The Origins of Methodism in the West Indies: The Story of the Gilbert Family," in *The London Quarterly Review*, January 1960, 185, pp. 9-17.

5. J. Wesley, *Journal*, IV, pp. 247-48.

6. Ibid, p. 292. The names *may* be Sophia Campbell and Mary Alley.

7. See J. Robinson Gregory, *A History of Methodism* (London: Charles H. Kelley, 1911), I, 180.

8. See Edgar W. Thompson, *Nathaniel Gilbert: Lawyer and Evangelist* (London: The Epworth Press, 1961).

9. Vaux, *Memoirs of the Life of Anthony Benezet*, p. 45.

10. Elmer T. Clark, ed., *The Journal and Letters of Francis Asbury* (Nashville: Abingdon Press, 1958), *Journal*, I, p. 149.

11. A splendid depiction of Methodism in the Caribbean in the late eighteenth century is found in John Vickers, *Thomas Coke: Apostle of Methodism* (Nashville: Abingdon Press, 1969), chapter 10, pp. 149-72.

12. Baker, "Methodism in the West Indies," p. 13.

Chapter VI Wesley's Comments on Slavery

1. J. Wesley, *Journal*, IV, p. 292.

2. J. Wesley, *Letters*, IV, pp. 292-93.

3. Ibid., IV, pp. 297-300.

4. Ibid., V, pp. 4-6.

5. Ibid., V, pp. 7-8.

6. J. Wesley, *Journal*, V, pp. 332-33.

7. Davis, *Slavery in the Age of Revolution*, p. 48.

8. J. Wesley, *Journal*, VI, p. 7. Also see Davis, *Slavery in Western Culture*, p. 382.

9. Davis, *Slavery in Western Culture*, p. 466.

10. See Paul B. Kern, *Methodism Has a Message* (Nashville: Abingdon-Cokesbury, 1941), p. 93.

11. See Outler, *John Wesley*, pp. 22-28.

12. See Warren Thomas Smith, "Our Wesleyan Heritage: A Social Conscience" (Atlanta: The Southeastern Jurisdictional Conference Council on Ministries, 1984), pp. 6-7.

13. See Warren Thomas Smith, "An Appraisal of Thomas Coke's Africa Mission, 1796–1811," in *Church History*, September 1971, Vol. XXXX.

14. J. Wesley, *Journal*, VI, pp. 277-78.

15. See Jackson, *Works*, VI, p. 345. The concluding sentence is again used by Wesley, ". . . are not these the works of thy own hands, the purchase of thy Son's blood?" in *Thoughts upon Slavery*, Section V, subsection 7.

16. J. Wesley, *Journal*, VII, p. 144.

17. Ibid., VII, pp. 359-60.

Chapter VII Benezet: A Quaker Opponent of Slavery

1. Also see James Walvin, *Black and White: The Negro and English Society 1555–1945* (London: Allen Lane the Penguin Press, 1973), chapter 7, "The Somerset Case, 1772," pp. 117-31.

2. See John S. Simon, *John Wesley the Master Builder* (London: The Epworth Press, 1927), p. 304.

3. See Baker, "The Origins, Character, and Influence of John Wesley's Thoughts upon Slavery," p. 79 ff. Also see Thomas B. Howell, ed., *State Trials* (London: Hansard, 1809–1828), 34 volumes, XX, pp. 80-82.

4. See A. F. Pollard, *Factors in American History* (New York: Macmillan Publishing Co., 1925), pp. 154-55.

5. J. Wesley, *Journal*, V, p. 445.

6. Ibid.

7. Ibid., V, pp. 445-46. ". . . that execrable sum of all villanies, . . ." is Wesley's preferred phrase to describe the slave trade. He employed it repeatedly.

8. Vaux, *Memoirs of the Life of Anthony Benezet*, pp. 2-3.

9. Ibid., p. 5.

10. Ibid., pp. 47-76.

11. See George S. Brookes, *Friend Anthony Benezet* (Philadelphia: University of Pennsylvania Press, 1937), p. 82.

12. Ibid.

13. Ibid.

14. Ibid., *A Caution and Warning to Great Britain*, p. 5.

15. Brookes, *Friend Anthony Benezet*, p. 447.

16. Ibid., p. 290. In Quaker fashion, the letter is dated "5th Month 14th, 1772."

17. Ibid., p. 291, from Wilson Armisted, *Memoirs of Anthony Benezet* (1859, rev.). See Baker, "The Origins, Character, and Influence of John Wesley's Thoughts upon Slavery," p. 78.

18. Brookes, *Friend Anthony Benezet*, pp. 418-19.

19. Roger Anstey, *The Atlantic Slave Trade and British Abolition, 1760-1810* (Atlantic Highlands, N. J.: Humanities Press, 1975), p. 240, quoting a letter from Sharp to Benezet, January 7, 1774. See Baker, "The Origins, Character, and Influence of John Wesley's Thoughts upon Slavery," p. 78.

20. Vaux, *Memoirs of the Life of Anthony Benezet*, p. 123.

21. Ibid., pp. 124-25.

22. Ibid., p. 136.

23. Manuscript at Perkins School of Theology, Bridwell Library, Southern Methodist University.

24. Said Brookes, "It is brimful of information concerning Guinea and its natives; a history of slavery from its beginning; a discussion of the conduct of

the slave trade; and finally, Benezet's own plan for the abolition of slavery."
Friend Anthony Benezet, pp. 83-84.
25. Benezet, *Historical Account of Guinea,* pp. i-iii.
26. Ibid., pp. 6-7.
27. Ibid., pp. 7, 11.
28. Ibid., pp. 1-3.
29. Ibid., pp. 31-32.
30. Ibid., pp. 138-39.
31. Ibid., pp. 141-42.

Chapter VIII Wesley's Thoughts upon Slavery, 1774

1. See Jackson, *Works,* XIV, p. 321.
2. See Albert C. Outler, ed., *The Bicentennial Edition of the Works of John Wesley,* vol. 1, *Sermons I, 1-33* (Nashville: Abingdon Press, 1984), p. 533.
3. See Baker, "The Origins, Character, and Influence of John Wesley's Thoughts upon Slavery," p. 80. His article is referred to throughout this chapter.
4. Davis, *Slavery in Western Culture,* p. 359.
5. Baker, "The Origins, Character, and Influence of John Wesley's Thoughts upon Slavery," p. 80.
6. See J. Wesley, *Journal,* I, p. 352, the diary entry for Tuesday, April 26, 1737, ". . . dined at Hugh Brian's," (or Bryan).
7. Wesley quoted this line on other occasions. The origin has yet to be found. See Baker, "The Origins, Character, and Influence of John Wesley's Thoughts upon Slavery," p. 81.
8. See Baker, "The Origins, Character, and Influence of John Wesley's Thoughts upon Slavery," p. 82. From an undated manuscript draft in Wesley College, Bristol, dated for its publication in *Wesley Banner,* 1849, p. 140.
9. See Anstey, *The Atlantic Slave Trade,* p. 240, quoting a letter from Sharp to Benezet, January 7, 1774.
10. Quoted in Brookes, *Friend Anthony Benezet,* p. 85. See also Davis, *Slavery in the Age of Revolution,* pp. 233-34.
11. Brookes, *Friend Anthony Benezet,* p. 447.
12. Manuscript in the Methodist Archives, Manchester.
13. From *Proceedings of the Wesley Historical Society,* XXXII, 45.
14. See D. D. Thompson, *John Wesley as a Social Reformer* (Freeport, N. Y.: Books for Libraries Press, 1971 [1898]), p. 47.
15. From *Monthly Review,* September 1774, pp. 234-37.
16. See Brookes, *Friend Anthony Benezet,* pp. 105-6. The "Run away" was "a Negro-fellow named Zeb, aged 36 years."
17. See Jackson, *Works,* XI, p. 81.
18. Ibid., XI, pp. 125-26.
19. Ibid., XI, p. 145.
20. See Baker, "The Origins, Character, and Influence of John Wesley's Thoughts upon Slavery," p. 85.
21. J. Wesley, *Letters,* VII, p. 195.
22. Ibid., p. 201.

Chapter IX Abolition of Slavery

1. See Davis, *Slavery in the Age of Revolution,* pp. 46-47.
2. A valuable study is Élie Halévy, *A History of the English People in 1815* (New York: Harcourt, Brace & Co., 1924).

3. See J. Wesley Bready, *England: Before and After Wesley, the Evangelical Revival and Social Reform* (New York and London: Harper & Brothers, Publishers, 1938), pp. 99-110.

4. J. Wesley, *Journal*, VI, p. 143.

5. Vaux, *Memoirs of . . . Benezet*, pp. 24-25. Also see R. Butterworth, "Anthony Benezet," in *Proceedings Of The Wesley Historical Society*, vol. 5, 1906, p. 40.

6. The official name: The Society Instituted in 1787 for Effecting the Abolition of the Slave Trade. See Davis, *Slavery in the Age of Revolution*, pp. 220-21.

7. J. Wesley, *Letters*, VIII, pp. 275-76, read to the Abolition Committee, August 21.

8. Ibid., VIII, pp. 6-7. Also see Thomas Clarkson, *History of the Rise, Progress and Accomplishment of the Abolition of the African Slave-Trade by the British Parliament* (London: Longman, Hurst, Reese, and Orme, 1808), I, pp. 447-48.

9. Clarkson, *History*, I, p. 83.

10. J. Wesley, *Letters*, VIII, p. 17.

11. Ibid., VIII, p. 16.

12. A splendid study of the economics of slavery during this period is Seymour Drescher, *Econocide: British Slavery in the Era of Abolition* (Pittsburgh: University of Pittsburgh Press, 1977).

13. Davis, *Slavery and Human Progress*, p. 109.

14. Élie Halévy noted, in retrospect: "In the vast work of social organization . . . of nineteenth-century England, it would be difficult to overestimate the part played by the Wesleyan revival." Cited in Bready, p. 403.

15. J. Wesley, *Letters*, VIII, p. 277. This letter was read to the Society on November 22, 1787. Of interest are Wesley's letter to Sharp, October 11, 1787 (copy in the British and Foreign Bible Society) and Sharp's letter to Wesley, November 14, 1787 (copy at Drew University).

16. Ibid., p. 23.

17. Ibid., p. 207.

18. *Minutes of the Methodist Conferences, Annually Held in America; From 1773) 1813, Inclusive.* Volume the First. (New York: Daniel Hitt and Thomas Ware, 1813), pp. 25-26.

19. See Baker, "The Origins, Character, and Influence of John Wesley's Thoughts upon Slavery," pp. 84-85, quoting from *Virginia United Methodist Heritage*, Fall 1977, pp. 27-28. Baker states, "Slavery is not in fact mentioned either in the printed *Minutes*, or in Haskins' manuscript for 1779."

20. See *Minutes*, 1773–1813, pp. 41, 46-47.

21. See Warren Thomas Smith, "The Christmas Conference," in *Methodist History*, vol. VI, July 1968, pp. 3-27.

22. See *Minutes of Several Conversations between The Rev. Thomas Coke LL.D. and The Rev. Francis Asbury and others, at a Conference, begun in Baltimore, in the State of Maryland, on Monday, the 27th of December, in the Year 1784, composing a Form of Discipline for the Ministers, Preachers and other Members of the Methodist Episcopal Church in America.* (Philadelphia: Charles Cist, M, DCC, LXXXV).

23. Also see Warren Thomas Smith, *1784 "I Remember the Christmas Conference . . ."*, adapted for drama by William S. Vance (Nashville: Abingdon Press, 1984), which seeks to capture the mood and spirit of the Conference.

24. See Warren Thomas Smith, "Thomas Coke's War on American Slavery," in *The Journal Of The Interdenominational Theological Center*, vol. II,

Fall 1974. Coke mentions a Captain Dillard, who though "as kind to his Negroes as if they were White servants," could not be convinced of the evil of keeping them in slavery "although he had read Mr. *Wesley's* Thoughts on Slavery, (I think he said) three times over: but his good wife is strongly on our side." *Extracts of the Journals of the Rev. Dr. Coke's Five Visits to America* (London: G. Paramore, 1793), p. 40.

25. Continued in *The Book of Discipline of The United Methodist Church 1984* (Nashville: The United Methodist Publishing House, 1984), p. 69.

26. For additional studies on slavery in American Methodism see Donald G. Mathews, *Slavery and Methodism: A Chapter in American Morality 1780–1845* (Princeton, N.J.: Princeton University Press, 1965), and H. Shelton Smith, *In His Image, But . . . Racism in Southern Religion, 1780–1910* (Durham, N.C.: Duke University Press, 1972). Also of interest, the biography of an important American black preacher, see Warren Thomas Smith, *Harry Hosier: Circuit Rider* (Nashville: The Upper Room, 1981).

27. J. Wesley, *Letters*, VIII, p. 24. The two lines of verse are quoted in *Thoughts upon Slavery*, Section V, subsection 7, from Charles Wesley's poem, "For the Heathen," third stanza.

28. J. Wesley, *Journal*, VIII, p. 35.

29. Ibid., p. 127.

30. Ibid., p. 128.

31. Vassa, *The Interesting Narrative of the Life of Olaudah Equiano*, II, pp. 77, 205. The first name is often spelled Olandah. Also see Emmanuel Obiechina, "Africa's Lost Generations," in *The Wilson Quarterly*, Summer 1981, pp. 178-87.

32. J. Wesley, *Letters*, VIII, p. 265.

33. Ibid.

34. Ibid.

35. Clarkson commented "the stain of the blood of Africa is no longer upon us . . . that we have been freed (alas, if it be not too late!) from a load of guilt, which has hung, like a mill-stone about our necks, ready to sink us to perdition." From Clarkson, *History of the Abolition of the Slave-Trade*, II, pp. 580-85.

36. On his retirement, Wilberforce spoke of "this Holy Enterprise . . . this *blessed service*." Wilberforce retired from Parliament in 1825. His work was carried on by others. He died in London, July 29, 1833, a month before the Emancipation Bill was passed. See Davis, *Slavery and Human Progress*, p. 145. The year 1807 saw the abolition of the slave *trade*; 1833, abolition of slavery itself, but with a period of transition. August 1, 1838, saw removal of all vestages of slavery and the end of the transition period.

37. James Morris, *Pax Britannica: The Climax of an Empire* (New York: Harcourt, Brace & World, 1968), p. 512. Also see Suzanne Miers, *Britain and the Ending of the Slave Trade* (New York: Africana Publishing Corp., 1975).

38. See Will and Ariel Durant, *The Age of Voltaire* (New York: Simon & Schuster, 1965), p. 136.

39. Ibid., p. 137.

INDEX